There are a number of HORIZON CARAVEL BOOKS published each year. Titles now available are:

BEETHOVEN
THE SEARCH FOR KING ARTHUR
CONSTANTINOPLE, CITY ON THE GOLDEN HORN
LORENZO DE' MEDICI AND THE RENAISSANCE
MASTER BUILDERS OF THE MIDDLE AGES
PIZARRO AND THE CONQUEST OF PERU
FERDINAND AND ISABELLA
CHARLEMAGNE
CHARLES DARWIN AND THE ORIGIN OF SPECIES
RUSSIA IN REVOLUTION
DESERT WAR IN NORTH AFRICA
THE BATTLE OF WATERLOO
THE HOLY LAND IN THE TIME OF JESUS
THE SPANISH ARMADA
BUILDING THE SUEZ CANAL
MOUNTAIN CONQUEST
PHARAOHS OF EGYPT
LEONARDO DA VINCI
THE FRENCH REVOLUTION
CORTES AND THE AZTEC CONQUEST
CAESAR
THE UNIVERSE OF GALILEO AND NEWTON
THE VIKINGS
MARCO POLO'S ADVENTURES IN CHINA
SHAKESPEARE'S ENGLAND
CAPTAIN COOK AND THE SOUTH PACIFIC
THE SEARCH FOR EARLY MAN
JOAN OF ARC
EXPLORATION OF AFRICA
NELSON AND THE AGE OF FIGHTING SAIL
ALEXANDER THE GREAT
RUSSIA UNDER THE CZARS
HEROES OF POLAR EXPLORATION
KNIGHTS OF THE CRUSADES

American Heritage also publishes
AMERICAN HERITAGE JUNIOR LIBRARY
books, a similar series on American history.
Titles now available are:

FRANKLIN DELANO ROOSEVELT
LABOR ON THE MARCH, THE STORY OF AMERICA'S UNIONS
THE BATTLE OF THE BULGE
THE BATTLE OF YORKTOWN
THE HISTORY OF THE ATOMIC BOMB
TO THE PACIFIC WITH LEWIS AND CLARK
THEODORE ROOSEVELT, THE STRENUOUS LIFE
GEORGE WASHINGTON AND THE MAKING OF A NATION
CAPTAINS OF INDUSTRY
CARRIER WAR IN THE PACIFIC
JAMESTOWN: FIRST ENGLISH COLONY
AMERICANS IN SPACE
ABRAHAM LINCOLN IN PEACE AND WAR
AIR WAR AGAINST HITLER'S GERMANY
IRONCLADS OF THE CIVIL WAR
THE ERIE CANAL
THE MANY WORLDS OF BENJAMIN FRANKLIN
COMMODORE PERRY IN JAPAN
THE BATTLE OF GETTYSBURG
ANDREW JACKSON, SOLDIER AND STATESMAN
ADVENTURES IN THE WILDERNESS
LEXINGTON, CONCORD AND BUNKER HILL
CLIPPER SHIPS AND CAPTAINS
D-DAY, THE INVASION OF EUROPE
WESTWARD ON THE OREGON TRAIL
THE FRENCH AND INDIAN WARS
GREAT DAYS OF THE CIRCUS
STEAMBOATS ON THE MISSISSIPPI
COWBOYS AND CATTLE COUNTRY
TEXAS AND THE WAR WITH MEXICO
THE PILGRIMS AND PLYMOUTH COLONY
THE CALIFORNIA GOLD RUSH
PIRATES OF THE SPANISH MAIN
TRAPPERS AND MOUNTAIN MEN
MEN OF SCIENCE AND INVENTION
NAVAL BATTLES AND HEROES
THOMAS JEFFERSON AND HIS WORLD
DISCOVERERS OF THE NEW WORLD
RAILROADS IN THE DAYS OF STEAM
INDIANS OF THE PLAINS
THE STORY OF YANKEE WHALING

A HORIZON CARAVEL BOOK

CONSTANTINOPLE
CITY ON THE GOLDEN HORN

By the Editors of
HORIZON MAGAZINE

Author
DAVID JACOBS

Consultant
CYRIL A. MANGO
*Professor of Byzantine Archaeology
Dumbarton Oaks, Harvard University*

*Published by American Heritage Publishing Co., Inc.
Book Trade and Institutional Distribution by
Harper & Row*
SECOND PRINTING

Library of Congress Catalog Card Number: 78-81403
Standard Book Number: (trade edition) 8281-5003-6; (library edition) 8281-8003-2
© 1969 by American Heritage Publishing Co., Inc., 551 Fifth Avenue, New York, New York 10017. All rights reserved under Berne and Pan-American Copyright Conventions.
Trademark CARAVEL registered United States Patent Office

FOREWORD

For centuries the inlet called the Golden Horn and the city on the hills overlooking it were situated in the middle of the known world. To the south, through the Dardanelles and the Aegean Sea, lay the Mediterranean, around which the Greek, Roman, Persian, and Arab worlds revolved. To the north, through the Bosporus, lay the Black Sea, with its Russian and eastern European coastline. And across the narrow Bosporus was Asia Minor, bridge to the Orient. Because of its strategic location, the city on the Golden Horn was coveted by a succession of different peoples. But even though it frequently was under siege, even though control of it often changed hands, and even though, indeed, it was conquered and leveled more than once, the city proved to be virtually immortal.

Founded nearly twenty-seven centuries ago as the Greek colony of Byzantium, the city was harassed by the barbaric Thracians, attacked by the Persians, vied for by the Athenians and Spartans. Weakened and dispirited, its citizens finally were forced to seek the protection of Rome, and the city became little more than a Roman outpost. Then, in the fourth century, the Roman Emperor Constantine I decided to build his capital on the site. It was in the new city of Constantinople that ancient Greco-Roman culture was married to Eastern Orthodox Christianity and that Western civilization became Christian civilization. As the center of the vast Byzantine Empire, the city was one of the richest and most important on earth. But because of its wealth, it was sacked by the Crusaders in 1204. And because of its strategic location, it was conquered by the Ottoman Turks in 1453.

Since then, as the Moslem city of İstanbul, it has remained an international metropolis, a city of East and West, a city whose great paintings, mosaics, statuary, and architecture reflect the many cultures that have been centered there and the many ages the city has survived. Along with modern photographs, the wealth of art work in İstanbul complements the tale that follows, a biography of a city in the middle of the world.

THE EDITORS

Seated in a kiosk, Turkish Sultan Ahmed III enjoys a 1720 water festival outside İstanbul. To rhythms supplied by musicians in boats, four boys dressed as women click castanets and dance across the Sea of Marmara. The horse, driver, and passenger in the daring aerial act are, alas, puppets.

RIGHT: *Carved in Constantinople in the fifth century, the figure on this ivory diptych panel is a personification of the city.*
KUNSTHISTORISCHES MUSEUM, VIENNA

COVER: *A tenth-century mosaic in Hagia Sophia depicts Emperor Constantine presenting a model of his new capital to the Virgin.*
BYZANTINE INSTITUTE INC., WASHINGTON, D.C.

FRONT ENDSHEET: *Surrounded by priests and soldiers, Emperor Justinian holds a votive offering in a sixth-century mosaic at Ravenna.*
SAN VITALE, RAVENNA: SCALA

TITLE PAGE: *This silver-gilt pendant, depicting St. Eusthathius, was made in Constantinople in the eleventh or twelfth century.*
DUMBARTON OAKS COLLECTION, WASHINGTON, D.C.

BACK ENDSHEET: *On another wall of the San Vitale church, Ravenna, a mosaic depicts Justinian's wife, Theodora, and her retinue.*
SAN VITALE, RAVENNA: SCALA

CONTENTS

	FOREWORD	6
I	THE DEATH OF A CITY	10
II	BYZANTIUM	26
III	NEW ROME	48
IV	THE CITY OF JUSTINIAN	66
V	THE CHRISTIAN CAPITAL	82
VI	SEAT OF EMPIRE	96
VII	CITY OF THE SULTANS	118
VIII	ISTANBUL	136
	ACKNOWLEDGMENTS	148
	FURTHER READING	149
	INDEX	150

I

THE DEATH OF A CITY

For seven weeks the citizens of the Christian city of Constantinople had been living with the sounds of their own coming devastation. They had listened to the whistling of cannon balls arching toward them, to the steady boom of artillery bombarding the city walls, to the noise of stone and rubble crashing to the ground. They had heard the constant clatter of flapping sails, announcing the presence of enemy ships in the waters around the peninsula on which their city was built. They had been awakened by the revelous cries, distant but nonetheless bloodcurdling, of the infidel warriors, the Ottoman Turks, who were encamped nearby. A tense and terrified people who needed no reminders of their danger, they had been reminded of it continuously.

Then, abruptly, on May 28, 1453, after several days of particularly intense, particularly noisy destruction, the siege of Constantinople stopped. For one of the few times in nearly two months, day broke quietly. No whistle, boom, or crash, no flapping clatter cut across the warm morning breezes. Even the Moslem troops were still.

Accustomed as they had become to destruction's noises, the people had good reason to be suspicious as they woke up on that sunny May Monday. Their own silence as they waited for the unfamiliar quiet to be shattered must have made the morning stillness ever stiller. But when no noises came, and they realized that the siege of their city indeed had stopped, the citizens of Constantinople began to replace the silence with sounds of their own making.

As all the churchbells began to ring, families poured out of their houses and called to the friends and relatives

The might of Islam was symbolized by the crossed swords on the banner of Mohammed, above.

The French miniature opposite depicts the Turks' cordon around Constantinople in 1453. To secure the inner harbor, the invaders built a land road for boats and a bridge of barrels over which to transport supplies.

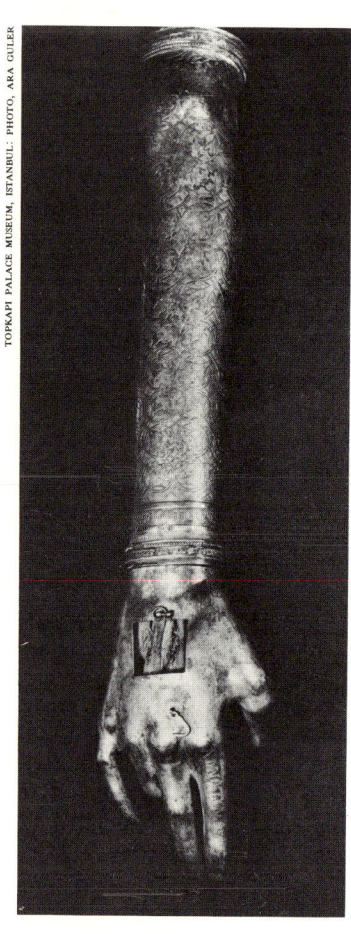

One of the last treasures created in Christian Constantinople was this gold reliquary, which is said to contain a bone from the hand of St. John the Baptist.

they sighted. Together, old and young, nobleman and beggar, priest and thief formed a grand procession through the narrow, hilly streets. At each of the many churches on their route the marchers stopped: several would enter, pray, and come out carrying high and proudly on their shoulders the sacred relics and icons that they had found inside. All day long the procession grew more impressive with the addition of these colorful artifacts. All day it grew more tuneful as the marchers sang their favorite hymns. Every now and then one of the priests would call a temporary halt to the march and chant a prayer. Every so often an important figure—a government official, a military leader, a foreign diplomat, even the Emperor himself, Constantine XI—would arrive, make a brief, sometimes moving speech, and march along for a while.

As the sun sank lower in the afternoon sky, the procession moved on toward the most famous landmark in Constantinople: the church called Hagia Sophia—"Holy Wisdom." It was the spiritual center of the Eastern Christian world, yet most of the pious people of the city, and most of the local religious leaders as well, had not entered the sacred shrine in more than five months.

The year before, when the threat of an imminent Ottoman invasion had become apparent, Emperor Constantine had appealed to the Christians of the West for military assistance. Most of the European leaders had been unresponsive, and the few who, pressured by Pope Nicholas V, had offered help had demanded a costly repayment: The Emperor had been required to agree to the unification of his Eastern (Greek) Orthodox Church with the Roman Catholic Church. Constantine had had no choice, even though he knew that the union would appall his subjects, who were Orthodox. The two churches had been united officially at a ceremony in Hagia Sophia on December 12, 1452. The residents of Constantinople had been so much offended by the appearance of Roman clergy in Roman vestments chanting Mass in the Latin language that thereafter they had refused to enter their beloved church. Their resentment of the West had increased in the months that followed, since the promised military assistance had arrived only in very modest quantity.

But on this Monday in May, 1453, all bitterness was forgotten. The local people and the European soldiers embraced each other and entered Hagia Sophia together. Standing side by side at the altar were bishops of both churches, taking turns chanting the sacred Liturgy in Latin and Greek. Worshipers took Holy Communion from Roman and Greek priests alike, without bothering to notice which was which. The Emperor, his ministers, and their allies arrived; having apologized to one another for past insults and injustices, they prayed together—not as Romans and Greeks bound by treaty, but as Christians bound by faith and blood brotherhood.

A stranger arriving in Constantinople on May 28, 1453, might well have thought that he was witnessing a joyous celebration. Clearly, the ringing bells, the grand procession, the speech-making, praying, and demonstrations of good fellowship were the sounds and sights of a momentous occasion. But if the stranger had taken part in the events and moved among the people, he would have seen how wrong his first impression had been. He would have realized before long that what he was attending was a wake.

The people knew their enemy. They knew that the determined young Ottoman Sultan, Mehmet II, had stopped the siege not because it had failed, but because it had been successful. It had wearied the defenders and weakened the city walls. It had broken the spirit of the Christians and resigned them to their fate. His silence told Constantinople that Mehmet now was ready to strike and destroy. The people knew that the Sultan was giving his well-prepared, battle-primed warriors a day of rest before committing them to the final assault. The Christians knew that the Turks were as confident of victory as they, the besieged, were sure of defeat.

Knowing all this, knowing that many of them would die along with the city, the people of Constantinople did not want to wait until after the city's fall to hold their wake. They mended damaged friendships, marched, sang, and prayed, hoping to attract the attention of God. Not all expected a miracle, but they hoped that He would at least see them ending their lives the way they thought that they should have lived them.

Outside the city walls, Sultan Mehmet was both calm and concerned. He was calm because he knew that he was going to win. He had planned long and carefully and had been faithful to his plans. When, during the siege, he had seen great vulnerable holes open in the city walls, when invasion appeared easy, when his men were anxious to take advantage of a breach and to pour through it then and there, he had restrained them. He had wanted to formulate a strategy to cover any eventuality: invasion on the spur of a moment would have made that impossible. He had in-

As the people of Constantinople marched in procession, praying for the salvation of their city from the Turks, they may have carried the bronze cross pictured above.

sisted on following his plans, not his impulses, and he had done his homework well.

But Mehmet also was wise enough to respect his enemy. He understood that planning and strategy could not always offset the courage and tenacity of opponents who would be defending not only a military fortress but their homes and families as well. More importantly, he was concerned because the moment itself dictated concern, earnestness, even reverence. The capture of Constantinople had been a goal of Moslems for almost as long as there had been Moslems. Although he was just twenty-one years of age, Mehmet appreciated the fact that he was the commanding officer of a generations-old army that was on the brink of achieving an objective of eight centuries. Solemnity seemed appropri-

The fifteenth-century engraving at left—attributed to the Florentine master Antonio Pollaiuolo—probably was not a portrait from life, but rather the artist's idea of what Sultan Mehmet II looked like.

ate on the eve of so significant a moment for Islam, the spiritual nation of all Moslems.

Young as he was, Mehmet undoubtedly realized also that the following day would be the climax of his own life: however long he might live, he would not likely surpass the moment for which he had planned so carefully. To say simply that he had lived for this moment would be an understatement; he had, in fact, lived for little else.

His dreams of conquest had filled a youth that was otherwise empty. His father, Ottoman Sultan Murad II, had, in the manner of many Islamic monarchs, kept many wives in a harem with branches in several cities of his empire. Mehmet, born in Adrianople on March 30, 1432, was Murad's third son; but while the mothers of his two elder half-brothers were noblewomen, Mehmet's mother once had been a slave. Officially, this made no difference in Mehmet's status: he was no less a prince because of it. It did, however, make a difference in Murad's attitude toward him. Murad, who favored his noble-born wives over his humbler ones, favored their children accordingly. For the first eleven years of his life Mehmet had grown up virtually ignored by his father.

The death of Murad's oldest son in 1437 moved Mehmet a step closer to the royal inheritance, and in 1443 the other heir was mysteriously murdered. At the age of eleven Mehmet thus became the probable successor to his father as Sultan of the Ottoman Turks.

Because of Murad's previous neglect, Mehmet had had little of the education appropriate to a prince. The Sultan therefore summoned many of the most prominent scholars and teachers in the Middle East to instruct the boy in the arts and sciences. As though making up for lost time, Mehmet devoted all his energy to his studies. Within a year he had become an astonishingly well-rounded scholar in his own right. His knowledge of history was thorough. He quickly digested the principles of military strategy. He became a man of letters, acquainted with ancient philosophies, well versed in the literature of many cultures. A distinguished writer, he also could speak six languages fluently. Tutored by his father, he effortlessly mastered the basics of government. So expert did he prove himself in the arts of administration and statesmanship that after only one year at court he had convinced his father that he was ready to help govern. Murad thus left most of the affairs of state to the talents of his twelve-year-old son and his tutor and began a relaxed semiretirement.

As a reigning prince, Mehmet revealed how deep were the scars of his childhood. Embittered by the years of neglect, he always had been mistrustful, secretive, and cynical —a loner. This he remained. He kept almost entirely to himself. He dined alone, made decisions alone, and if he relaxed at all, relaxed alone. He had no friend, expressed no confidences, welcomed no suggestions, accepted no advice. He ignored the ministers of his father's court. He was educated but was unable to apply his knowledge to human affairs. He knew, for example, that a ruler must be firm yet benevolent, but he could not easily tell the difference between occasions that demanded firmness and those that required benevolence. As a result, to the distress of his father's advisors, he was capable of ordering the execution of a pack of petty thieves and then pardoning a band of murderers. One day he might reject as meaningless reports of activity that anyone else would recognize as signs of a coming attack on the borders of his empire. The next day he would be recommending the immediate invasion of Constantinople.

The constant complaints of his ministers and the grumblings of his subjects drew Murad back to Adrianople on several occasions, but until 1446 he was satisfied with Mehmet's performance. In that year, however, the army's discontent with their youthful commander and the possibility of a military uprising against him convinced the Sultan to resume control. The experience proved beneficial to Mehmet, who first was exiled for two years and then brought back honorably to participate in several military campaigns. The period of exile provided valuable time to think out the mistakes that he had made; he would not make them again. The military experience provided valuable battlefield training. Both the patience he had learned and the tactics he had studied would serve him well.

Murad died on February 13, 1451. There was no doubt that Mehmet would become Sultan, but he was taking no chances. His father had had one other son, an infant whose mother was a noblewoman. Arriving at Adrianople, Mehmet sent a court official to kill the child. At the very moment when the mother was congratulating the new Sultan on his coronation, her son was being drowned in his bath. Then the official who had done the deed was executed at Mehmet's order. Another command decreed that the

Like the prince in the Persian manuscript opposite, young Mehmet was surrounded by more experienced and supposedly wiser heads when he commanded his father's court; but the decisions of a ruler were his alone to make.

16

Covered with pious inscriptions, steel and silver helmets like this were worn over the turbans of the Turks assaulting Constantinople.

mother marry a government official to whom Mehmet had given a position in Asia Minor. With the only threats (or imagined threats) to his position—a half-brother and his father's most distinguished widow—out of the way, Mehmet took over the throne and concentrated on capturing Constantinople.

Murad II, like many Ottoman sultans before him, had posed a perpetual threat to the peace and well-being of Constantinople. After all, the capture of the Christian city long had been a Moslem goal, for it was the gateway to power in the West. Leaders bent on retaining their influence in Islam had to speak the words and make the gestures that foretold the imminent doom of the Christian infidels who occupied the ancient city.

With the rapport that sometimes develops between traditional foes, however, Emperor Constantine gathered that Murad would rather not launch the major attack that would be needed to take the city. Constantine knew that he could not let down his defenses or in any way make it easy for Murad to invade, but he felt that if he prepared himself with fortifications and alliances and revealed no weaknesses, Murad probably would not move against his capital. Despite periodic crises, the Emperor's impression proved true.

Now Murad was dead, and Constantine knew enough about the new Ottoman Sultan to realize that the uneasy peace was over. At first the Emperor may have underestimated the strength and skills of his new enemy, perhaps remembering Mehmet's problems as reigning prince some years earlier. But soon Constantine acted with the proper sense of urgency by appealing to the West for help and by reinforcing as best he could the defenses of his grand but decaying city. Unfortunately, the European leaders also seemed to have underestimated the young Sultan's intentions and abilities and therefore withheld the support that Constantine desperately needed.

In any case, Mehmet had few problems in preparing for the assault. Constantinople was situated on the tip of Thrace, the European peninsula that tapers from the Balkans and reaches out toward Anatolia, or Asia Minor. Both Thrace and Anatolia belonged to the Ottoman Empire, and the Sultan was able to establish operations wherever he wished in order to encircle the city.

In the summer of 1452 Mehmet built a massive fortress on the Bosporus shore. From there he was able to control the waters north of the city. Early the next year he moved his men into encampments on Thrace, behind the city walls and across the Golden Horn—the inlet of Thrace that served as Constantinople's harbor. Then he sent for the Turkish armada, which arrived through the Dardanelles into the Sea of Marmara to the south of the city, through the Black Sea and Bosporus to the north and east of the city. Thus did the narrow waterways in the middle of the world, the waters separating Europe from Asia, the waters that had made the city overlooking them one of the most important on earth for some two thousand years, fill up with the ships of Sultan Mehmet.

Early in 1453 the Genoese sent several hundred men, under the command of a capable general, Giovanni Giustiniani Longo, to help in the defense of Constantinople. The Genoese, however, were concerned mainly with the suburb of Pera, which was a Genoese colony, and Constantine could not be certain that Giustiniani's men would devote their total energies to the salvation of the city. Nine Venetian ships also were at port in the harbor. They were converted into warships and their commanders agreed to help defend the city "For the honor of God and the honor of all Christendom." The only remaining hope that Constantine entertained was that help would come from Europe. Constantine's hope may have been fed by reports of Europeans traveling eastward in substantial numbers.

The reports were true. But the Europeans were not coming to defend Constantinople. They were mercenaries, and they were on their way to work for the Sultan. The arrival of the mercenaries bolstered Mehmet's forces, which have been estimated at more than eighty thousand men.

The siege began on April 6. Two weeks later, the Turkish onslaught was sidetracked when three large Genoese galleys and an imperial transport appeared in the Marmara bearing provisions and ammunition. Reacting promptly, Mehmet dispatched a fleet of one hundred forty small, oar-driven boats to stop the vessels. But on the windy day in the rough waters of the Bosporus Strait, the lightweight boats had difficulty in navigating, and the sailors on the larger ships bore down on them, ramming and sinking many. From the decks of their vessels the Genoese sailors threw rocks at the Turks and made fire bombs, which they flung into the Ottoman boats.

Late in the afternoon the wind died down briefly, and the supply ships drifted helplessly toward Pera. Taking advantage of their enemy's sudden lack of maneuverability, the Turks launched an attack, setting fire to the hulls and attempting to board the vessels. The Christian sailors de-

In the struggle for Constantinople, both armies were bolstered by mercenaries, such as these, depicted in a Neapolitan chronicle.

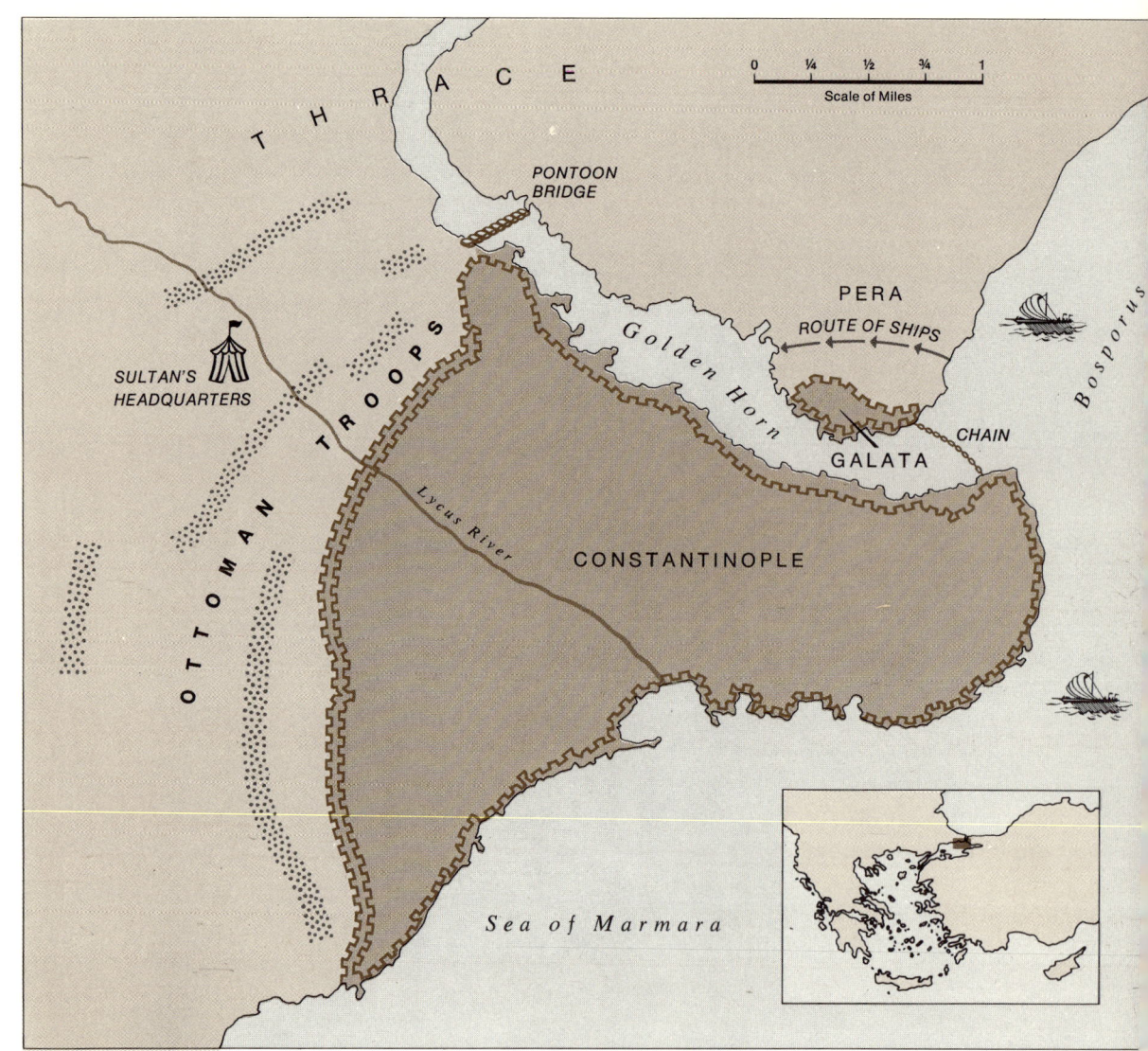

As Mehmet surrounded Constantinople, possession of the Golden Horn eluded him. A chain blocked the entrance to the harbor and kept the Turkish fleet from entering. But the Sultan devised a plan to move his ships from the Bosporus overland, behind the suburb of Galata, and seize the harbor from within. It worked: the city was doomed. At upper left, the map shows the site of the pontoon bridge built of barrels by the Turks.

fended themselves brilliantly, extinguishing the flames and repelling all who tried to board. But by evening, the exhausted, damaged ships seemed ready to capitulate. Suddenly, the breezes blew up again; the sails billowed full, and all four ships cruised safely into the Golden Horn.

Watching from horseback on shore, Mehmet was beside himself with rage. He even had driven his horse into the water, so furiously had he been spurring on his sailors. Unfortunately, it is not known what measures the Sultan took against his unsuccessful admiral, Balta Oghlu. One story relates that Mehmet slew the officer himself; another, that he had the men beat the admiral to death with sticks; and

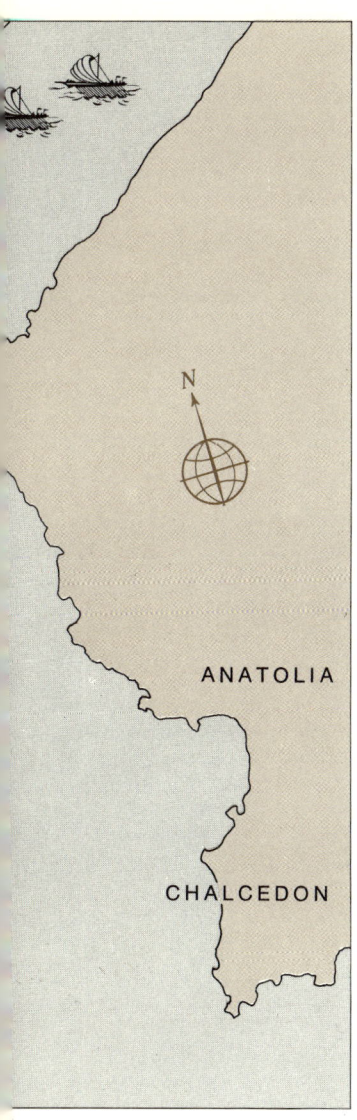

still another, that he pardoned him. Whatever punishment he may have given, however, Mehmet resolved to suffer no more setbacks.

On April 22 Mehmet, in his determination to capture the Golden Horn, treated the Christians inside the city to a strange sight. The Bosporus entrance to the inlet was flanked by two hills, each with towered walls. Fastened to each wall was an end of a huge length of chain, which extended across the entrance to the inlet, just under the surface of the water. Ships entering the harbor were halted effectively by the chain and vulnerable to bombardment from the towers; thus, this approach was out of the question. An attack by land might have worked, but for the proper occupation of a harbor ships are needed, not men.

Mehmet's solution was ingenious. First he ordered a road built from the Bosporus over the land north of the city, around the suburb of Pera, to the Golden Horn. Huge rope cradles were made and fastened to wooden bases on metal wheels. These cradles were sunk in the water beneath the large ships, and pulleys were used to drag the ships ashore. The rope was tied to teams of oxen, and with the help of the men, the boats were hauled across the road. Their sails flapped as usual. Their crews sat in place and oared against thin air. Flags were raised, and the musicians played the music of sailors going to battle.

After the Christian leaders in the city recovered from the shock of sighting this peculiar procession, they assembled to try to plan resistance to the Turkish takeover of the harbor. Unfortunately, they delayed for six days: not until April 28 were the Venetian and Genoese ships that were docked at Pera released for combat. By this time, the Turks had secured their artillery on shore. Although the Christians fought fiercely and well, Turkish numbers and firepower were overwhelming; and soon the Italian and Greek vessels in the harbor were either fleeing or sinking.

At one point during the battle, forty Christian sailors from a sinking ship swam to shore and were captured and executed while the city watched. Retaliating, the citizens brought all the prisoners they had captured—two hundred sixty of them—to the walls of the city, and while the Turks looked on from below, beheaded them one by one.

When the bloodletting stopped, the Golden Horn belonged to Mehmet. To secure the harbor, he built a pontoon bridge—constructed with about one hundred wine barrels. The bridge made it possible for the Moslem troops to cross from one side of the harbor to the other quickly, moving men and cannon to where they were needed most. From then on, Christian Constantinople was living on borrowed time. On May 28 the Sultan decided that its time was up. He examined the breaches in the city walls, reviewed the strategy, and gave his men a day of rest.

Monday night it rained, and the people inside Hagia Sophia wondered if this was a sign that the miracle they had been praying for had come. The rain stopped, and the people prayed on. Midnight came. One A.M. passed quietly. Constantinople was as still as it had been at daybreak.

At one-thirty on Tuesday morning a terrifying chorus of battle cries arose from outside the walls, and the bells of Constantinople started ringing again. All the men and many of the women rushed directly to the walls to try to stop the attackers. The old people and young children and their mothers who had gone home now returned to the churches. Amid clanging bells, gunfire, screams, and the roars of battle they prayed again for a miracle.

Thousands upon thousands of Turkish irregulars—mostly the European mercenaries—armed with swords, bows and arrows, even slingshots, scaled the walls and pounded on the gates. Coaxing them on from behind were Mehmet's police, ordered to kill any who wavered. Few from the front lines penetrated the defense, but they kept trying, endlessly, for two hours. Then Mehmet sent word to withdraw. They had not entered the city, but they had done their job according to Mehmet's plans; they had been meant not to break the defense but to exhaust the defenders.

Within minutes the siege began anew, and this time an army of Anatolian Turks stormed the walls. Fighting almost until dawn, they were no more successful than the mercenaries. But just when it seemed as though the Greeks had repulsed this second wave, a Turkish cannon struck the wall at a particularly vulnerable spot, and the wall tumbled. Only three hundred men rushed through the gap, however, for the defenders quickly closed in on them and made a stopper out of their bodies.

The Sultan had hoped that the Anatolians would succeed, but he had not counted on it. Giving the Christians no more than a few minutes of relief, Mehmet, who had offered a reward to the first soldier through the walls, ordered forward his own elite troops, the Janissaries. After an hour the Janissaries themselves began to weaken, so great was the defense. But the toll of the night's fighting began to tell on the Christians. The warrior Giustiniani was shot and removed to the inner city. Many of his men, thinking the

After they captured Constantinople, the Turks intensified their efforts to extend their empire beyond the Balkans and into eastern Europe. The ferocity and determination of their warriors forged a series of victories that eventually took them as far west as Vienna. Above, under Sultan Suleiman, they vanquish a Hungarian cavalry at the Battle of Mohacs in 1526.

The miniature above, from a Byzantine manuscript, depicts men of Constantinople praying in Hagia Sophia. In accordance with Eastern Orthodox tradition, an icon—sacred image—hangs on the wall.

battle lost, followed and left the gate of the inner wall open. Gaps in the walls were widened. Gates were pounded down. More and more Turks poured through. Now the battle was lost.

Emperor Constantine, having pleaded vainly against Giustiniani's leaving his post, looked around at the chaos. There were Turks everywhere, and the Christian warriors, who had defended the city so nobly for so many hours, were climbing over one another to flee from the invader. Looking around at the hills of his capital, he saw the Ottoman flag flapping from a tower. He removed his royal insignia from his apparel and flung himself into the legions of infidels and to his death.

The people still were packed into Hagia Sophia. They knew what was happening. They heard the Turks straining against the gates. They heard the metal gates crashing to the ground. They watched the infidels storm through the sacred portals. Trapped, surrounded, the horrified Christians huddled in a mass toward the center of the church. The very old, the very young, the crippled, the fear-frozen —all were murdered where they stood. Groups of invaders moved toward the noblemen and toward the prettiest girls, argued over possession, and tore their victims to pieces. Garments were ripped off the prisoners and used to tie them together so that they could be dragged back to the soldiers' quarters, where they would be divided up for sale as slaves. Priests still praying at the altar prayed on until they were stopped by a blow on the skull or a sword through the throat.

Late Tuesday afternoon Sultan Mehmet entered the old church. Noticing one of his men hacking away part of the building, he admonished him: looting, he said, was acceptable, but looting did not mean destroying. A few remaining citizens and priests came out from hiding places and begged for mercy. Mehmet spared them and sent them home protected by his personal guards. Then he gestured to his *ulema*—a Moslem holy man—who approached the altar. "There is no God but Allah," proclaimed the *ulema*, "and Mohammed is His Prophet!" Mehmet repeated the proclamation, and kneeling, said his prayers.

At that moment the church called Hagia Sophia ceased to exist. The grandest edifice in all Christendom had become a *mosque*, a Moslem house of worship. And the Christian city of Constantinople ceased to exist, too.

But soon the new Moslem city—İstanbul—would restore life to the remains of Constantinople. It would rise importantly, overlooking the waters in the middle of the world. It stands there still, behind the Golden Horn, which has been the site of a great city since history's earliest days.

Below are the ruins of the walls built around Constantinople by the Byzantine Emperor Theodosius II in the fifth century. The once-unassailable walls finally were breached in 1453, when the Ottoman Turks under Sultan Mehmet the Conqueror captured the city.

25

II

BYZANTIUM

The early Greeks knew the north wind by the name of Boreas. He lived, according to their lore, in the hills of the land called Thrace, an extension of the Balkan Peninsula. Violent and vengeful, he periodically departed from his home to vent his anger in distant places, but always he came back to Thrace. It was an angular, craggy country, unfertile and in places parched. The climate was given to extremes of hot and cold, although even a heat wave could be interrupted by—without necessarily being relieved by—fierce and unpredictable gusts of wind. The seas around the land and the rivers running through it were tempestuous, crashing constantly against the shores. Little grew there. Goats ran wild on weather-stripped hillsides.

Boreas had subjects in his kingdom, the only kind of people who could be subjects of the despotic wind. They had been in Thrace from earliest times—since the Stone Age, probably—and they ran with the goats. Their skin was olive-tan, and they tattooed almost every inch of it. In structure their society was tribal, but the tribes were small and savage, resembling, the Greeks observed, packs of wolves. They had a religion of a sort, but one whose gods demanded frequent sacrifice of human flesh. Their language was similar to that of the Illyrians, another Balkan people who painted themselves and who, like the Thracians, were regarded by the Greeks as uncivilized—scarcely above the animals.

The Greeks might never have become involved with the Thracians if it were not for the geography of the peninsula. By design or accident, Nature had carved a small incision, an inlet, at the tip of Thrace. Because of it—because of

Above, an agent of Boreas chases two harpies and a sphinx—notorious kidnappers in Greek legends.

Throughout its stormy history the city of Byzantium was host—willing or not—to a succession of visiting troops. At left is a wall painting from the fourth century B.C. showing how Greek warriors dressed at that time.

27

what might have been nothing more than a slip of Creation's gouge—the Thracians could not keep civilization indefinitely from their shores. For although they did not know it, the inlet at the end of their land was a strategically situated gateway to every part of the known world.

Early Greek history, which often is difficult to separate from Greek mythology, is very much concerned with the problems of exploration—and with the search for sites for cities. This is reflected in the legends of the Mycenaean Greeks: the stories of the Trojan Wars, the voyages of the Argonauts, the rise and fall of Thebes, Argos, and Troy. Assuming that such stories as those on which the *Iliad* and especially the *Odyssey* were based were to some extent true, we can be reasonably certain that Mycenaean navigators traveled as far north as the Black Sea well before the twelfth century B.C. One indication of this is the fact that that difficult body of water had been named by the time recorded history of the region began. Characteristically, the Mycenaeans, who were strong believers in the power of wishful thinking, called it the Euxine, or "Hospitable," Sea: perhaps they hoped that by calling a treacherous sea hospitable they would attract the attention of the gods, who then would make it hospitable in fact.

The more certain history of the lands and seas south of

The Dorian Greeks were fine navigators, but the risks of sailing through uncharted seas were formidable. Understandably, the passengers depicted on the black-figure vase above are ecstatic at having reached land safely.

the Euxine begins with the Ionian and Dorian Greeks in the seventh century B.C. Around 685 B.C. a group of settlers from the Dorian city-state of Megara arrived in the Sea of Marmara in order to establish a colony. From this base Megara hoped to exploit the riches of the Euxine area—silver and copper, timber and rare species of cattle and grains not available in the Mediterranean region, and a substantial variety of fish.

It was clear to the Megarians that the best location for their settlement was the land flanking the Bosporus. From the shores of the strait the Euxine was accessible, shipping into and out of the sea could be controlled, and vessels approaching through the Marmara from the south could be seen and dealt with. Less clear, however, was the question of which side of the Bosporus was better for a colony. Both the Thracian and Anatolian sides offered something of value. For what seemed to them to be sound reasons, the Megarians chose Anatolia, and there they built the city of Chalcedon.

The Megarians probably selected Anatolia because the current around it was gentler than that of the Thracian site, the land was more level for building, and there were no barbaric Thracians to contend with. Nevertheless, the site did not prove to be a fortunate one, and the riches that Megara had expected to gather never materialized. Ships from the Ionian city-state of Miletus negotiated the Bosporus into the Black Sea and established colonies, and the Megarians were unable to collect tolls or taxes. Moreover, in a showdown—if ever one should be necessary—the Milesians probably would prevail, for the Megarian hold on the strait was too tenuous to be meaningful.

Around 658 B.C. another wave of Megarian colonizers arrived in the Bosporus. Criticizing their predecessors, they nicknamed Chalcedon The City of the Blind: only blind men, they reasoned, could have failed to see the advantages of the Thracian side of the strait.

Hindsight, of course, made criticism easy for the later settlers, but the tip of Thrace was definitely a better location for a city than the tip of Anatolia. True, the winds and currents around the Thracian peninsula were strong, but they could be used to advantage to virtually pull vessels into the inlet and usher them out. Behind the inlet were a series of hills that provided ideal vantage points from which all navigation in the Marmara could be closely surveyed. The hills also protected the inlet from all but the most unconventional storms. From the inlet the actual gateway

MUSEO ARCHEOLOGICO, FLORENCE

29

into and out of the Bosporus from the Marmara could be reached much more quickly than from the port of Chalcedon. Given its location and its values for commercial shipping and for military control of the waters, it is no wonder that the inlet presently would be named The Golden Horn—golden for its worth, horn for its distinctive ram's-horn shape.

Little is known about the arrival of the second fleet of settlers. It does not seem likely, however, that they were welcomed by the tattooed natives of Thrace. There are some indications that the Thracians made it so difficult for the settlers that the Megarians, Milesians, and even smaller groups of settlers from elsewhere shared the wall-building chores.

For a century the Greeks had little opportunity to test the value of their site. Most of their time was spent building walls. The walls grew higher and stronger, but the Thracians scaled them anyway. They had developed into expert raiders and looters, at times even boarding the ships in the Golden Horn and carrying off the cargoes. Late in the seventh century, however, some of the settlers managed to call a truce and to arrange a peace talk. With what must have been elaborate ceremony (of which both the Greeks and the Thracians were fond), the colonists met with a Thracian prince and began negotiations.

An agreement was reached more easily than anyone had expected. The Greeks would establish a real city behind the Golden Horn, and the Thracians would be welcome to participate in the municipal government. The city would be named for a god with whom both Greeks and Thracians were familiar. His name was Byzas, and he was the son of Poseidon, god of the sea. Thus was the city of Byzantium born and named. The Thracians returned to their homes in the hills, and the Greeks began to plan a city to fill in the land within the walls.

Not long after the ceremony, a pack of Thracians descended on Byzantium and wrecked and looted, and things returned to normal. As before, the principal enterprises of the settlers were wall building, wall strengthening, and wall rebuilding.

The situation was not without its benefits, however. Apparently, conventional building techniques were inadequate to erect walls of sufficient size and strength to repel the determined Thracians; thus the Byzantine Greeks became extremely skillful wall builders. They cut their stones to fit squarely into one another, and no joints were visible.

As Greek commerce expanded, so too did the number of Greek colonies. On the sixth-century-B.C. cup above, the king of Cyrene, an African colony, supervises preparation of flax or hemp for export.

Rising above the walls were seven towers extending in a row from the Thracian Gate in the south to the Golden Horn. For purposes of communication, the builders deliberately placed these seven towers according to an acoustical plan that made a sound a struck gong, for example —echo successively from one tower to the next.

Very, very slowly, as the walls became more difficult for the Thracians to breach, some measure of organization began to work its way into the structure of the city. The instability of life there, however, made it difficult for Byzantium to retain a constant population. Rivalries divided the people according to where they came from—Miletus or Megara or someplace else—and some citizens recognized no home city. Governments were formed and usually were ignored and dissolved in rapid order. The Town Council, composed of what passed for the nobility (whoever was richest at the moment), had a constant turnover of mem-

In the fitness-conscious Greek world the foot race—pictured above on a vase from the fifth century B.C.—was one of many scheduled athletic competitions.

bership. The People's Assembly, representing the populace, seldom had more than token power.

The culture—such as it was—of Byzantium was basically Greek, but the city produced no important figures in science, art, music, literature, or drama. Charlatans and swindlers, fortune tellers and magicians abounded and prospered, however. Although the government sponsored an annual torch race, the Bosphoria, which achieved some widespread fame, it was the ceremony and not the quality of the event that distinguished it: early Byzantium sent no winning athletes to the Olympic Games. Farmers and herders who came to try to develop the surrounding countryside were quickly discouraged when Thracian tribes raided their crops or stole their cattle. Notwithstanding its splendid location, then, Byzantium remained until 500 B.C. a well-built, well-protected city having little purpose for its strength and containing little that was worth defending.

In the meantime, a formidable foe was beginning to look in the direction of the Bosporus. He was Darius I, the Persian king, master of the largest realm on earth.

Around 512 B.C. Darius had secured much of Thrace. Soon after the turn of the century he was at war with Athens. Plotting his strategy, King Darius saw what the Megarians had seen two centuries before: that control of the Bosporus was equivalent to control of the Black Sea, which was the northern perimeter of the known civilized world. Therefore, in 497 B.C., while he planned to lead an army across the Mediterranean to mainland Greece, he sent one of his ablest military men, General Otanes, to capture Byzantium and Chalcedon. Most of the citizens of the twin cities on the Bosporus never had seen such an armada as the one that approached their shores. As news of the impending invasion spread, the people, who had had their fill of troubles anyway, promptly developed a defensive strategy: they would run away. And they did.

For awhile in 497 the Persian troops relaxed in the empty cities. The self-exiled citizens, seeing the enemy entrenching himself, converged on the northern coast of Thrace, and fighting the Thracians as usual, started building a new city: Mesembria.

Almost from the start, Darius' wars against the Athenians went badly. In 490, while preparing for the forthcoming Battle of Marathon (which would be disastrous for the Persians), Darius sent for the army of General Otanes. Before they left the twin cities on the Bosporus, however, the Persian troops took care to remove anything of value that could be carried, destroy everything of value that could not be carried, and set the rest on fire. Chalcedon was virtually leveled. Byzantium's walls, for the most part, remained in place, but they protected nothing.

Certainly the city was not much of a prize; nevertheless, in 477 the Spartan warrior Pausanias led an armada into the Golden Horn and took possession of Byzantium. He had plans for the city—grandiose plans. He intended to use it as a tool with which to achieve a one-man rule of all Greece —with himself, of course, as the one man.

Pausanias had had a taste of power two years earlier and had not liked giving it up. In 480 a cousin of his had inherited the leadership of Sparta. But the cousin was far away fighting the Persians, and Pausanias had been appointed guardian of the throne. When relieved of these responsibilities, Pausanias had been placed in command of all the allied forces of Peloponnesus and Athens—probably a force in excess of one hundred thousand men. With very little delay the warrior forced a confrontation with the Persians in Boeotia, and he won decisively and with a minimum of losses to his own men. As a reward for this victory, he was allotted ten per cent of the spoils, including a tenth of the recaptured territory. Then, early in 477, Pausanias led an allied Greek fleet and drove the Persians out of the

The wealth and might of the Persians—symbolized by the sword of gold above—were challenged fruitfully by the Greeks in the fifth century B.C. Commemorated on the kylix at left, the epic struggle established the Greeks' dominance over the Mediterranean world.

This handsome bronze depiction of a Spartan soldier was created around 490 B.C. Such brave warriors helped to drive the Persians from Byzantium in 477 and to establish the city as a base for the ill-fated schemes of their self-proclaimed "king," Pausanias.

islands east of the Greek mainland. It was during this Aegean campaign that he decided to head north and secure the city of Byzantium.

Having occupied the Thracian city, Pausanias began to enact his plan. First he returned some of his Persian prisoners to their homeland in good health and sent a letter along with them. In it he asked for Persian aid in the formation of a Spartan-Persian confederacy, which would include all of Greece, provided he could be the ruler of the Greek regions. To seal the bargain, he proposed to marry a Persian princess. Persia naturally was eager to accept this opportunity to regain much of its dwindling empire.

When word of Pausanias' plans reached Sparta, the warrior, who had taken to calling himself King Pausanias, was recalled. During his trial he denied everything. Acquitted for lack of evidence, he returned to Byzantium to continue his plans. But rumors continued to fly, and Greek allies of the Spartans began to clamor for Pausanias' removal. Again Sparta recalled him, and again he was not convicted. The leaders could not prevent him from carrying on his conspiracy, either—first, because Byzantium belonged to him according to the spoils agreement, and second, because he was a member of the royal family with powerful friends and influence.

The plans of Pausanias and the Persians never materialized. As a matter of course, they had adopted the foolish precautionary practice of having all messengers bearing communications between them executed after delivery—just in case the messengers had read the notes en route. It was inevitable that the messengers themselves would begin to grow suspicious. One such messenger, bearing a note from Pausanias, wondered why none of his colleagues had returned from such missions. He opened the message and read it, uncovering not only the nature of the plans, but an order for his own execution as well.

Pausanias was in Sparta when the messenger arrived there to turn in the note to the Spartan authorities. An order for the traitor's arrest was sent out immediately; but somehow, Pausanias escaped, fleeing into the Temple of Athene Chalcioecus for refuge. It was Greek tradition not to arrest anyone in a holy place, but the Spartan leaders, who had no intention of letting Pausanias go free, had the portals blocked with stone. In a pompous ceremony, Pausanias' own mother laid the first stone at the door, condemning her son for treason. Several weeks later, the stones were removed to prevent the traitor's body from contami-

Well equipped and skillful, the Persians' archers had been instrumental in the capture of Byzantium in 479 B.C. The glazed tile mosaic above once adorned the ancient Persian palace at Susa.

nating the sanctuary. The timing was perfect: Pausanias was still alive, though barely. Emaciated from starvation, he staggered out of the temple and keeled over, dead.

The treachery of Pausanias had important consequences for the politics and geography of the time. Directly or indirectly, it stimulated the rise of the Athenian confederacy, and it was responsible for the rebirth of the city of Byzantium.

Exhilarated by their victories over the Persians, Sparta's allies (mostly cities and provinces in Peloponnesus and some in Attica) had been prepared to cast their lot with Sparta in the years after the wars. But Pausanias, who almost had started a new war, was a Spartan. That Sparta itself was not party to his conspiracy did not matter: Sparta had twice prosecuted Pausanias without convicting him, had allowed him to return to Byzantium to conspire again. Sparta's apparent helplessness during the affair, its inability to acquire incriminating evidence, its hedging on removing Pausanias from power, and its ultimate admission that he had been plotting all along did not improve its image among its allies. During the affair and even more so afterward, the less powerful city-states and regions found themselves drawn closer and closer to Sparta's rival in Attica, Athens. The episode, in fact, gave the formation of the Athenian confederacy its greatest boost.

The new population of Byzantium was composed partially of old residents returned from Thracian-looted Mesembria, partially of members of Pausanias' fleet, and partially of the usual adventurers, fortune-hunters, and disenchanted expatriates who usually settled Greek colony-cities. But these settlers were possessed of a much greater determination to make Byzantium survive than earlier settlers had been.

In 470 B.C., the year of Pausanias' death, Byzantium became an independent city-state affiliated with the Athenian League of city-states. A political party that favored an alliance with Sparta remained active in the structure of the city government, but the pro-Athens party continued to prevail. When the Athenians were defeated in a Sicilian war in 413, however, the Byzantines began to consider the possibility that a change might be in order. In 411 a famine overcame Thrace; Athens was too busy with its far-ranging wars to provide much help, and the pro-Spartan party was returned to power. Byzantium was precious to Athens, though: Athens' share of tolls from Bosporus navigation was an important source of revenue, and the Athenians de-

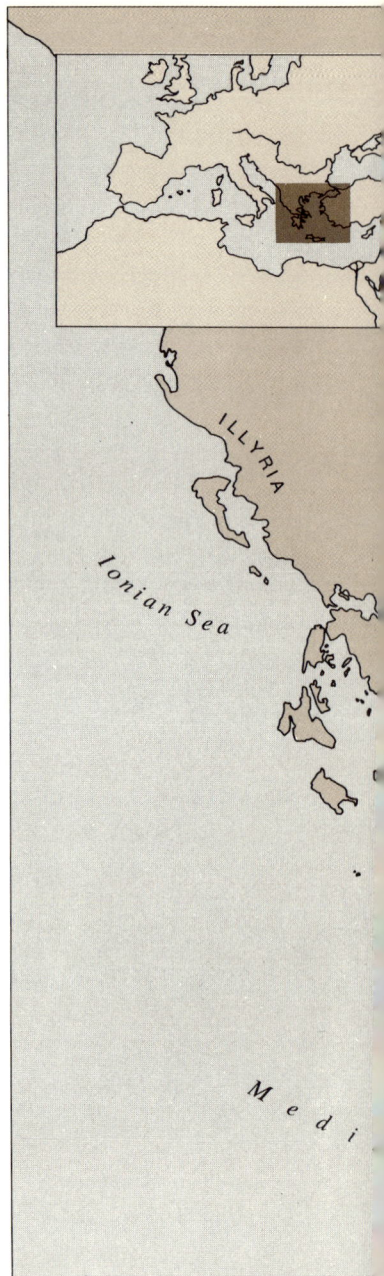

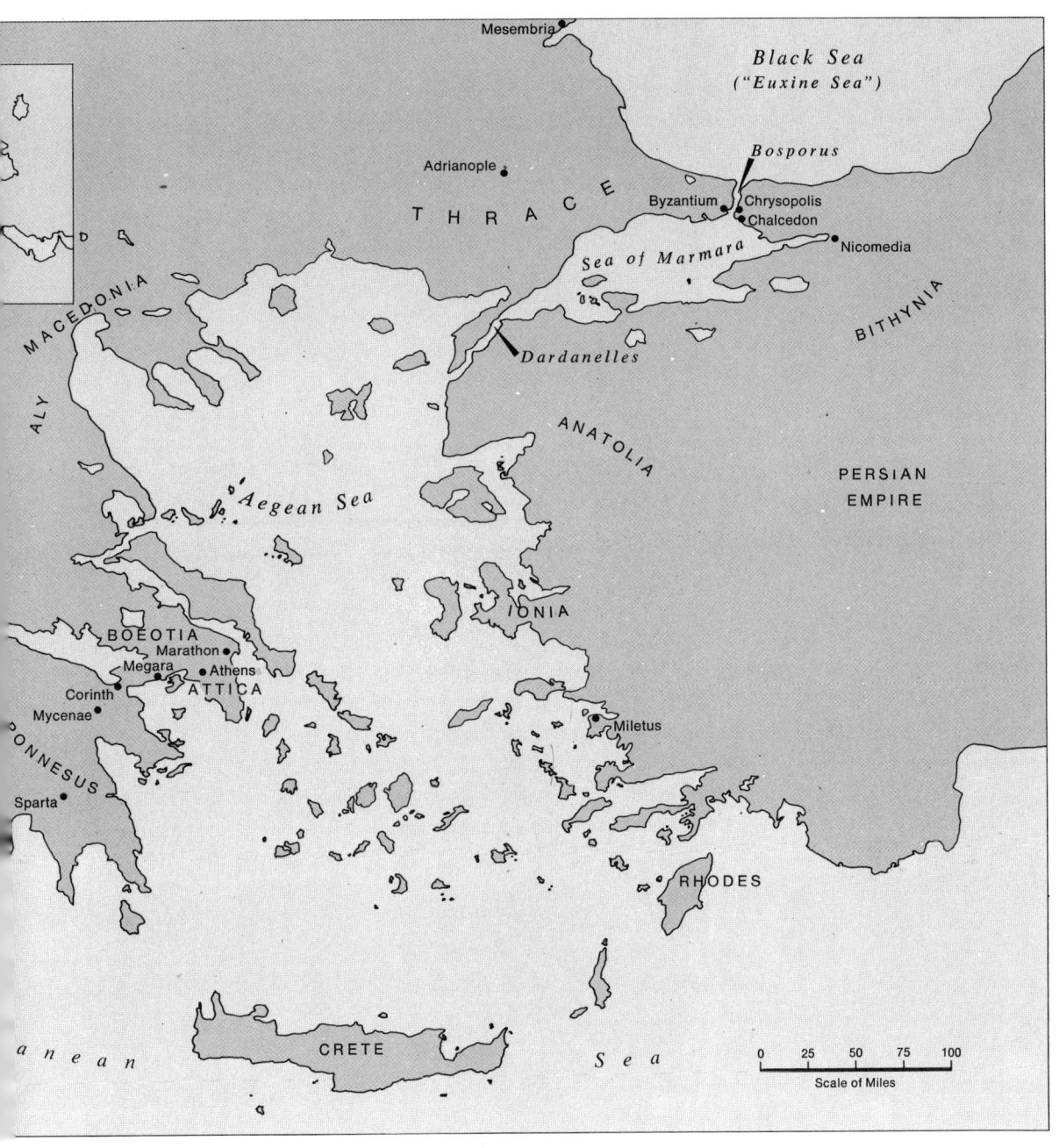

pended on wheat imported from the Ukraine by way of the Straits. In consequence, in 408 Athens sent the warrior Alcibiades, a student and friend of Socrates, to recapture control of the city.

The division that Alcibiades' arrival produced in Byzantium largely undid the progress of the previous sixty years. Brutal battles erupted in the marketplace between the pro-Sparta and pro-Athens factions, and not even Alcibiades, whose reputation for firmness and brutality was second to none in the Greek world, could calm the city. Finally, the leader managed to restore peace, but only by promising to retain the independent status of the city and to pardon all citizens who had opposed his arrival.

In 407 Alcibiades lost favor with the Athenian leadership when one of his officers was defeated in an important battle far away from Byzantium. A year later he prudently entered a voluntary exile from the Greek community. As soon as he left Byzantium, Spartan troops entered, and the same street fights and disintegration followed.

In 400 B.C., with the city in the hands of the Spartans, an army of Greek mercenaries arrived after a long journey from Mesopotamia. Their generals all had been killed there, and the soldiers themselves had elected a new leader —the Athenian Xenophon, another of Socrates' students. The men followed Xenophon as he led them overland along the Tigris, across Armenia, and down along the Black Sea coast to Byzantium, where they were welcomed by the resident Spartan admiral, Anaxibius.

Anaxibius was glad to see the mercenaries and told them so; he also offered them further mercenary service with his troops. Penniless and eager to return to their trade, most of the men enthusiastically accepted. Anaxibius immediately employed them on several missions but neglected to pay them. When Xenophon and some of the men inquired about their pay, the admiral instructed them to cross the Bosporus and collect their money and goods on the site of Chalcedon, where he maintained a fortress.

As soon as all the men left the walled city, Anaxibius closed and bolted the gates. Furious, the mercenaries turned on the city and began a sustained siege. The admiral had underestimated the mercenaries. They were not merely professional fighters; he himself had honed their skill with the missions on which he had sent them. Moreover, the people of Byzantium, believing the city lost, began to retreat to the harbor. As they opened the gates, the mercenaries stormed through and began destroying and looting. The whole city might have been leveled once again had not Xenophon called off his men. He talked with Anaxibius and secured the pay his men had worked for. Most of the troops departed then, leaving Byzantium intact. About four hundred remained, however, some to settle there, some indecisive about where to go next, some, perhaps, just vacationing. Unfortunately, Xenophon was among those who

The Macedonian king depicted on this ancient coin probably is Philip II, whose invading army was repulsed by the Byzantines with Athenian help in 340 B.C.

left. No sooner had he gone than Admiral Anaxibius arrested the four hundred and had them all sold as slaves.

During most of the fourth century B.C. Byzantium enjoyed comparative peace and prosperity and a substantial degree of independence from Spartan or Athenian control. Perhaps the most important event to guarantee that that independence would continue was the defense the citizens put up against the invading armies of Philip II of Macedon in 340 B.C. Led by a soldier-scholar named Leon, a student of Plato, the people held out against the persistent siege while a message was sent to Athens, asking for help. The Athenians did send help, but apparently they judged that the Byzantines themselves had been chiefly responsible for repelling the Macedonians and did not, as a result, try to claim control of Byzantium as a reward for saving it. The grateful Byzantines awarded special privileges to Athens, including some toll-free shipping through the Bosporus, on which they erected three statues showing the people of Athens being crowned by the people of Byzantium.

It was a symbolic gesture only. The Byzantine people were crowning no one but themselves; they had achieved, through their victory over the Macedonians, the dignity and respect that they long had wanted. Word of the defensive battle spread throughout the world. Philip went on to capture most of the Greek world, but he never again attempted to seize Byzantium.

Byzantium's good times were brief. In the third century B.C. the native Thracians began threatening once again. Now they were bolstered by another people, whom the Greeks called Red Thracians. They were actually the red-headed Celts, a nomadic barbarian people, who moved into Thrace and somehow arranged to live in harmony and cooperation with the Thracians. The Thracians and Celts did not destroy Byzantium, but their constant and bothersome attacks wearied and weakened the people at a time when they should have been getting stronger and more alert.

Around 280, Celtic bands sweeping across Thrace demanded unusually high tribute from the Byzantines, and the city was compelled to increase the toll charges for passage through the Bosporus. The Rhodians, whose briefly flourishing trade took them through the strait often, objected and in 219 went to war with Byzantium.

Rhodes did not attack Byzantium, but with its ally, Bithynia, took control of the Dardanelles and prevented all ships from reaching the Bosporus. Thus the Byzantines were compelled to abolish the high tolls, although the damage

39

to the city's prosperity and independence was irreparable. Rhodes remained in command of the Dardanelles, and the Celts increased their demands on the Byzantine treasury.

Throughout the first century A.D. the almost impoverished city repeatedly was compelled to ask the Romans—who had supplanted the Greeks as rulers of the ancient world—for help in defending itself and arbitrating disputes with its neighbors. Each time the Romans responded, Byzantium had to give up some of its privileges in return (the Romans were permitted free use of the city's facilities, for example). Gradually, Byzantium became a Roman protectorate, lethargic and weak.

In A.D. 73 the Roman Emperor Vespasian noted with contempt that the inhabitants of Byzantium had "forgotten to be free." Thus he officially removed Byzantium's independent status, declared it a Roman city, and assigned it to the province of Bithynia. There is no record of Byzantine resistance to the declaration.

A far worse fate befell the city in 196. Earlier in the decade control of the Roman Empire had been contested bitterly by Septimius Severus and Pescennius Niger. Neutrality was impossible in this struggle, and although the people of Byzantium tried their best to remain uninvolved, they favored Niger. In 193 Niger wanted to use Byzantium as his headquarters. To refuse him was to side with Severus; to allow him to enter the city was to side with him. With no middle road possible, the Byzantines admitted Niger.

When the struggle was won by Severus, he immediately decided to demonstrate how firm an emperor he would be. As a specimen, he chose Byzantium; he would teach it a lesson for supporting Niger. But Byzantium was not about to be taught a lesson too easily. For three years the people held out against the siege of Septimius Severus. No ships came into its harbors; no gates could be opened to allow people to go out for food.

In the summer of 196 the Romans entered Byzantium through a breach in the wall of three years' making. All local officials and soldiers were executed on the spot, and the citizens were sold into slavery. Severus later relented, renamed the city Augusta Antonia, and instituted a new building program. But the city on the Golden Horn was now little more than a Roman outpost. The Romans treated the Thracian scavengers who stole through the city streets like flies—sometimes ignoring them, sometimes swatting them. Architecture in the city was thoroughly Romanized; Roman coins were currency.

Diocletian and Maximian, above, were the two augusti *of the Roman Empire who ruled East and West in the third century* B.C.

Above is a portrait of Septimius Severus and his family. The obliterated face belonged to a son who was killed by his brother.

Its formidable size notwithstanding, the Roman Empire was not healthy at the beginning of the third century. Internal divisions were many, and corruption and apathy and complacency were rampant. Frequent changes in rulers had produced erratic shifts from the benevolent to the tyrannical.

There was no real rule regulating the succession of emperors, and in the half-century before A.D. 284, twenty emperors came and went, the average length of their reign about two and a half years each. The usual method of achieving the throne was rebellion, almost invariably engineered by the military. Under these circumstances, the Roman Senate was reduced to impotence, and the support of the people within the empire steadily dwindled.

In 284 Diocletian, a government official whose father had been a freed slave and who was known more for his administrative abilities than for his military skills, was elevated to the throne. Unlike his predecessors, he was bent not on securing his own personal power, but on reorganizing the administrative structure to make the empire manageable. He created a system called the tetrarchy in which administration of the realm would be divided into eastern and western halves, each with its separate ruler (*augustus*) and vice-ruler (*caesar*), who would take over upon the retirement of the *augustus*. The advantage of this arrangement

Byzantium was one of the countless ports between Britain and the Orient that were visited by the Roman merchant fleet, which brought goods from all over the empire back to Rome. In the relief sculpture below, a merchant ship returns to Ostia, the port of Rome. On its sails Romulus and Remus are shown being suckled by a wolf.

Four emperors are depicted in a stance symbolic of imperial unity on this medieval sculpture. Now housed at the church of St. Mark in Venice, the statue may have been carved in Constantinople. But it is not known whether the figures represent the four original rulers under the Roman tetrarchy or the sons of Emperor Constantine.

was that it prepared the way for a continuous turnover of leaders without the turmoil that usually accompanied a change of leadership. It also allowed the rulers to divide chores between two men (the *augustus* might concentrate on administrative matters, the *caesar* on military) while maintaining a clear hierarchy and succession.

To demonstrate the sincerity of his reforms, Diocletian himself gave up control of one half of the Roman Empire. He chose to rule over the eastern half and established his capital at Nicomedia in Anatolia. He appointed a warrior named Galerius to be his *caesar*. For the western half he designated Maximian *augustus* and Constantius *caesar*. In order to guarantee the smooth transition of governments for the future, Diocletian and Maximian agreed to abdicate at the end of twenty years.

The tetrarchy worked only as long as Diocletian and Maximian ruled. Not long after they abdicated in the year 305, a power struggle began that lasted six years. Of the many Romans competing for power, the sons of Constantius and Maximian—Constantine and Maxentius—prevailed and in 312 faced each other in a battle that would turn the tide of history—and of the evolution of the Christian religion.

Maxentius held Rome, and Constantine was strongest in Gaul and the southern Alps. After a stunning series of victories in the northern Italian peninsula, Constantine headed for the capital of the Western Empire.

The story is told that as Constantine approached Rome to meet the much more numerous forces of Maxentius, he was startled by a vision in the noonday sky: it was a glowing cross, and below it were the words, "By this conquer." Inspired and determined (the story goes), Constantine boldly charged into the army of Maxentius, which was so enormous that it seemed like a human wall on the banks of the Tiber. On the river itself more of Maxentius' troops were stationed on a bridge of boats. Constantine's Gallic army swept right and left, shoving aside the defenders as though it were a wolf and they a yard full of chickens. With his own small band of officers Constantine rode onto the bridge of boats, whose captains panicked and dispersed. Maxentius was driven off the Milvian bridge and drowned, and the rest of his army surrendered quickly. Constantine absorbed most of the soldiers into his forces. With his new, huge army, the *augustus* was virtually all-powerful. Declaring his ally Licinius *augustus* of the East made it so, although in essence he, Constantine, was the Roman Emperor.

In 314 war broke out between Constantine and Licinius, and Constantine won, adding, in consequence, Illyricum and Greece to his half of the empire. He allowed Licinius to remain *augustus* of the East, however, probably because they were brothers-in-law. (Constantine's sister Constantia had married Licinius in 313.) Nine peaceful years followed, but in 323 tensions were brought to bear again. For Licinius the mistake and the resulting battle would be fatal. The mistake was that he began excluding Christians from his court.

Prejudice against Christianity was nothing new in the Roman world. The young religion had been a thorn in the

This gold medal commemorates a 313 meeting of the augusti *Constantine and Licinius in Milan.*

BIBLIOTHEQUE NATIONALE, PARIS

44

The ninth-century miniature opposite depicts the events that led to the widespread acceptance of Christianity. In the top panel, Constantine dreams that the sign of the cross will lead him to victory in his coming battle. In the center panel, he defeats Maxentius at the Milvian bridge near Rome. At the bottom his mother, Helena, discovers the True Cross in the Holy Land. Only a few years earlier, Emperor Diocletian had ordered a Roman soldier, Sebastian, executed for converting to Christianity. At right, a fifteenth-century Spanish painting depicts the martyrdom of Saint Sebastian.

side of imperial Rome since its inception, one of the internal challenges to which the government had failed to respond successfully. Indeed, the reforms of Diocletian might have gone even further than they did if he had not abandoned his tolerant attitude toward the sect and wasted so much time and energy trying to eliminate the Christians from his realm.

But of course, Constantine's conversion changed everything. And yet, the details of the conversion are elusive.

It is possible that Constantine actually did think that he had seen a glowing cross in the sky. Some historians have pointed out that he always had been an extremely competent but extremely conservative general and that his head-on assault on the huge forces before Rome was wholly out of keeping with his normal tactics. Something extraordinary, real or fancied, they claim, must have inspired him, and the attack was daring enough (or lucky enough) to have succeeded.

Yet it is also true that Constantine had sound, political reasons for affecting a personal conversion to Christianity. In some quarters the religion already had achieved a degree of respectability, and almost everywhere it was acknowledged to be a growing force in the world. There were several "official"—or tolerated—religions in the empire, and Constantine might have thought that Christianity should have been added to this list. Because the Christians had generated such fierce and long-time hatred within the government, however, the *augustus* may have concluded that his ministers would not tolerate a simple proclamation of its acceptability. It would not have been out of character for him to have devised a very personal, unchallengeable way to introduce Christianity into the scheme of Roman life, particularly if he found most of its theology to be attractive.

Whatever the case, Constantine adopted the cross as a standard, made Christianity an officially tolerated religion of the empire, and became a Christian himself. When Licinius began his exclusions in 321, however, Constantine disapproved but did nothing more. After a year or so, the Roman Emperor requested a halt in the persecutions in somewhat stronger language, but Licinius only increased his arrests. In 323 the issue came to a head, but probably it was Licinius' defiance of his orders, rather than the persecutions themselves, that made Constantine react.

Licinius' armies were driven from Adrianople, Chrysopolis, Byzantium, and finally from his capital, Nicomedia. The war took only about three months. Licinius was saved from execution only because Constantia begged for his life, but he was banished to Thessalonica. In 324 it was rumored that the exiled *augustus* was meeting with barbarians and providing them with information regarding the best way to invade the empire; and Constantine had him executed.

Now Roman Emperor in name as well as function, Constantine came to a major decision as a result of the war of 323. He would move his capital to the East.

Rome and the West were pagan places. Constantine wanted not only a newly defined empire, but a Christian empire as well; and the East, with its longer tradition of monotheism, mysticism, and indeed, absolutism, would be more receptive to the idea.

When he had led his armies against Licinius, Constantine had been struck by the beauty and potential impregnability of the poor little city of Byzantium. He had been thinking about a site for his new capital—Serdica and Troy apparently had been foremost in his mind—and Byzantium became a likely candidate. It was true that it was not in very good shape at the time. Swarms of Goths lately had pounded the city almost to rubble. But Constantine was not looking for a city that was already beautiful. He was looking for a site on which to build a beautiful city—the capital of a new Christian empire, his city.

The Emperor returned to Byzantium in 324 and set a stone in place: here would rise, he said, Christianity's own city, the capital of Christianity's own empire. He named it Nea Roma—New Rome. But it would be known as the city of Constantine—Constantinople.

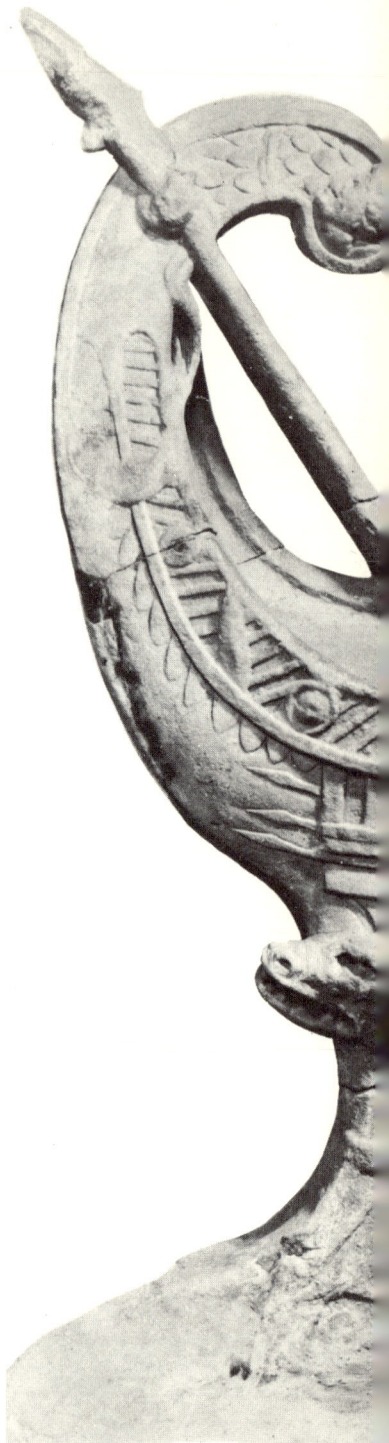

MUSEO VATICANO, ROME

It must have required many ships similar to the war galley above to transport Emperor Constantine and his entourage to his new capital on the site of Byzantium. The galleys were rowed by slaves from all over the empire.

BIBLIOTECA VATICANA, ROME

III

NEW ROME

According to legend, Constantine himself indicated the location of the huge wall that would protect his new capital. He stood, one day in 324, on the south Thracian shore, about two miles west of the peninsula's tip. Dramatically, he lifted his spear, extended it ahead of him, and began to pace slowly inland, tracing a wide arc well beyond the existing boundaries of the city. The Emperor's aides, the story continues, were alarmed by the wide sweep of his path and finally inquired: "How much farther, Sire?" Constantine's reply was: "Until he who walks before me stops walking."

Along the curved path that Constantine, divinely inspired, had traced, a wall was built: it enclosed five of the seven hills at the end of Thrace, and it defined a city four or five times larger than Byzantium. Within the walls, Constantine ordered built a number of splendid churches, public buildings, houses, and a fine palace for himself. Only the barest outlines of the great city that Constantinople would become, however, took shape during Constantine's lifetime: the city's founder died in 337. The brevity of his reign at Constantinople notwithstanding, Constantine had established a city, an empire, a civilization the importance of which would be hard to overstress.

And yet Western Christians sometimes are guilty of underrating the significance of the Eastern Christian world. The truth is that Western civilization evolved from several sources and that some of the most vital elements in its roots might have been lost if Constantine had not established his empire in the East. Most Westerners, for example, freely acknowledge that their cultural ancestors were the Greeks

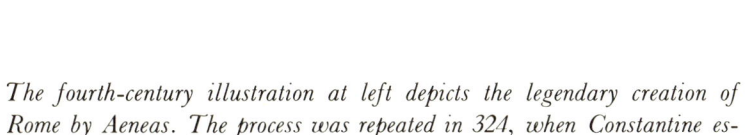

Minted in 330, this coin commemorated the founding of Constantinople, the new Roman capital.

The fourth-century illustration at left depicts the legendary creation of Rome by Aeneas. The process was repeated in 324, when Constantine established "New Rome" at Byzantium and supervised the city's construction.

The bronze portrait bust of Emperor Constantine, right, was cast in his lifetime, probably in Constantinople.

and Romans of antiquity. They also think of themselves as descendants of the ancient Hebrews and early Christians who suffered slavery and were fed to lions by oppressors. But few among them recall that they also are the offspring of the barbarian hordes that wandered through Europe two thousand years ago and descended on Rome soon after Constantine's departure.

When, in the fourth and fifth centuries, the barbarians overran the Western Roman Empire, they were exposed to and in a superficial way assumed the Romans' fashions and culture. They also adopted Christianity. But while Christianity influenced the development of the barbarians' society, it is no less true that the barbarians' customs and even pagan beliefs influenced the shape of Christianity. Tribes were ordered to become Christian: if anyone expressed doubts or resistance, he might be tortured or executed according to age-old barbarian tradition. Pagan gods sometimes were converted, virtually overnight, into Christian saints. The result in the West was a harsh, repressive kind of Christian civilization, and the era was called—rightly or wrongly—the Dark Ages.

The traditions of Classical Greece and Rome—traditions of ethics, art, law, and language—indeed were absorbed into Christian civilization. But it was the Eastern Empire established by Constantine, not the West, that provided the main repository for these traditions. Certainly, barbarians and barbarian influences seeped into Constantinople and particularly into the outer extremes of the Eastern Empire. But the East more than the West retained the riches of Classical culture.

The chief importance of New Rome, then, was that it was at the same time capital of the Roman Empire and of a realm that would become the first Christian empire. There, in Constantinople, Classical civilization evolved into a Christian civilization.

Although neither Constantine nor his sons witnessed the flowering of their Christian empire, the evolution of the new civilization centered in Constantinople was, according to history's clock, remarkably swift. It took only about two hundred years for all the divergent elements that migrated to Constantinople to meld into the population that would become the strength of the Byzantine Empire.

In Constantine's day the aristocracy of his capital consisted principally of transplanted Romans and provincial gentry. Their arrival with money to spend and their quest for profitable ways to invest it sent land values soaring. As a result, some native Byzantines who owned tracts of land in or near the city were potentially rich men. In characteristically Roman fashion, however, the administration of Constantinople was soon under the control of a complicated bureaucracy; and if the local landowners were not careful, they found their property heavily taxed or even confiscated and their potential profit lost. Nevertheless, those who were shrewd—or lucky—became the new aristocracy of the city.

The rich of Constantinople demonstrated their status by maintaining both a townhouse within the walls and a villa in the suburbs—on the Bosporus shores at first and later on Exokionion, the seventh hill of Constantinople, which had been situated outside the city walls. These aristocratic families tended to become very clannish, insulated, and self-protective. Each maintained its own court and re-

The Ostrogothic bird-and-cross above shows how the Christianized barbarians combined their traditional art forms with the symbols of their new religion.

tained resident tutors, scholars, priests, and entertainers.

Not very highly regarded in the Middle East, and somewhat patronizingly honored in Rome, women were at once carefully protected and treated as intellectual equals in Constantinople. Young girls were kept at home until their marriage and taught spinning, weaving, sewing, and other conventional feminine skills. They often were given the same academic training as their brothers, but not university educations. Once married, a woman enjoyed the social and intellectual freedom of men; and she was permitted by law to own property—an innovation in that part of the world.

Like Rome, Constantinople was dominated by a coalition of churchmen and property owners. There were, however, fundamental differences in the division of power as it developed in East and West, and these differences produced important variations in the way of life in each empire. The Christianized barbarians were inclined to centralize power: the pope was for many years the *de facto* king of an empire, and the bishops were aristocratic landowners who also led troops in battle. The Byzantines, on the other hand, made a greater distinction between secular and religious functions. Education, for instance, was never, as it was in the West, considered the responsibility of the Church. The ancient Greek idea of secular education was highly valued, and the Classical-style education—which emphasized Homer, Aristotle, and the great orators; taught science as philosophy; and had only a secondary regard for technology—was prized. An elaborate apprenticeship system trained young professional men; and all physicians, engineers, and architects were expected to train students.

Constantinople quickly became one of the world's great commercial cities. Caravans and ships laden with raw materials, luxury goods, and exotic gems and spices came from every direction in a steady flow. Rows of warehouses were built along the Golden Horn to contain the goods. Artists, craftsmen, scribes, and manufacturers, including jewelers, cosmeticians, weavers, and tanners, converged on the city, along with wanderers looking for work.

Commerce not only provided Constantinople with much of its early color, but it also reflected how much the customs of the city were blends of East and West. In Western fashion, members of each major profession were inclined to organize into guilds. The government saw the guilds as a stabilizer of the city's economy and structure and both encouraged and regulated their growth. In fact, a guild member's sons were required by law to follow in their father's profession.

The actual way that commerce was conducted, however, was recognizably Oriental. Merchants and craftsmen dealing in similar goods tended to bunch together; the major ones—jewelers and dealers or weavers of fine fabrics, for instance—occupied their own streets. As a rule, the shops flanked an arcade or forum and were very small, for most businessmen liked to work alone or with an apprentice and one or two child helpers. In warm weather the commercial area of the city became a cluster of awnings and pavilions—a great colorful bazaar almost continuously crowded and busy. In the Oriental manner, vendors chanted about the quality of their goods, and the air was filled with singsong descriptions of copper candlesticks and fine linens.

The air of Constantinople also was filled with the smells of fresh food being cooked on charcoal fires in the many taverns and outdoor eating places that were situated along the streets. Mixed in among the stalls and shop-front displays were little food stands where shoppers could sample

Although the miniature below depicts an Old Testament scene—the meeting of Joseph and Potifar's wife—the costumes are typical of those worn by Byzantine aristocracy in the sixth century.

In the markets of Constantinople produce was weighed on scales similar to the one above: the hooks gripped the purchase and the bulbous weight was moved to the correct indicator. The bronze figures of empresses shown below were used as weights on other scales.

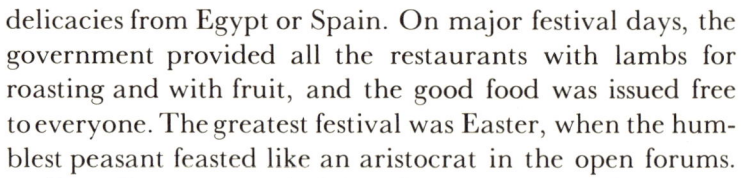

ALL: DUMBARTON OAKS COLLECTION

delicacies from Egypt or Spain. On major festival days, the government provided all the restaurants with lambs for roasting and with fruit, and the good food was issued free to everyone. The greatest festival was Easter, when the humblest peasant feasted like an aristocrat in the open forums.

But all was not colorful and prosperous in Constantinople. Slavery, a holdover from pre-Christian times, not only survived, but also was approved of by the Church, which itself owned slaves. (The Church did, however, emphasize the necessity of treating slaves humanely and set up elaborate codes defining the responsibility of master to slave and slave to master.) Slaves were protected to some extent by law—a mistreated slave was permitted asylum in the churches—but for the most part remained at the mercy of their owners.

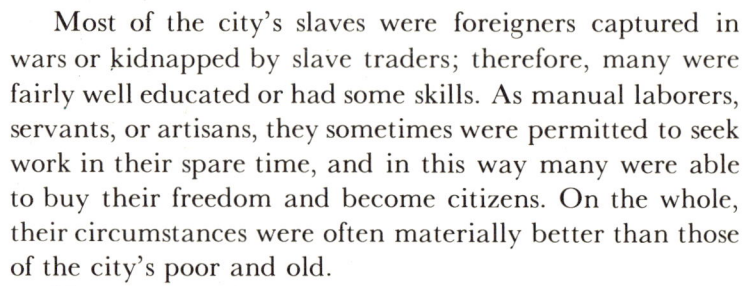

Most of the city's slaves were foreigners captured in wars or kidnapped by slave traders; therefore, many were fairly well educated or had some skills. As manual laborers, servants, or artisans, they sometimes were permitted to seek work in their spare time, and in this way many were able to buy their freedom and become citizens. On the whole, their circumstances were often materially better than those of the city's poor and old.

Not until the Renaissance would the West become as enlightened toward the problems of the poor as was the Byzantine government as early as the fourth and fifth centuries. By today's standards, the Byzantines might not be regarded as particularly compassionate, but they did, for their time, have a remarkable sense of responsibility toward the victims of poverty. The government built a number of homes for the aged and orphaned, several public hospitals, and poorhouses that were not like prisons. In the larger churches free meals were served daily, and both Church and State felt some obligation to provide jobs for the unemployed. The poor often could find work on government building projects, and sometimes maintenance jobs were available in the churches.

The emperor in Constantinople generally assumed the responsibility for supplying his subjects with bread. At times it was issued free to all, but almost always it was given without charge to the city's poor. Many of the people depended on the bread for their very existence. The grains, however, had to be imported from abroad. Egypt was the major supplier until the seventh century; several different countries provided the grains thereafter. Occasionally, the grain ships were delayed, and more than once the failure of the grain to arrive before the supply of bread was exhausted led to riots in the streets.

As was the case in ancient Rome, the Byzantine government assumed the responsibility for providing the people with entertainment. Most popular of all was the circus, housed in a gigantic arena, the Hippodrome, next to the royal palace. The favorite circus event was the chariot race, and when one was held, the emperor and his court would join the sixty thousand people in the Hippodrome to encourage their favorite drivers.

The emperor often had more than a sporting interest in the outcome of the chariot races. As in Rome, there usually were four vehicles in each competition—one red, one green, one blue, and one white. In Constantinople each chariot represented one of the civic factions called demes, whose leaders (demarchs) were members of the city administration. The demes were, in an autocratic state, the nearest thing to a democratic element, for their influence was based on their popularity among the people. Each deme had its own militia, which could be and often was mobilized to defend the city—but which also represented a reminder to the emperor that the people had rights and the means with which to secure those rights.

By the sixth century, the demes had become an accepted part of the life of the city of Constantinople. The Reds and the Whites had died out as political forces—although they still entered chariots in the races—and the Blues and the Greens occupied the sections of seats in the Hippodrome flanking the box of the emperor. Almost as a matter of course, the two factions opposed each other on every issue, and fights in the arena or in the streets were not uncommon. Both parties, however, fancied themselves the spokesmen for all the people.

The members of the Blue and Green parties were pompous, vain, and flamboyant. They dressed in billowing cloaks

"As Consul I offer this to my Fathers"—so says the medallion on the ivory diptych above, commissioned by Justinian in 521.

and capes and tunics of many bright colors. While most men of the time were clean-shaven and had short hair, these peoples' spokesmen wore mustaches and beards and let their hair grow very long in back. It was not uncommon for bands of demes to highjack caravans and rob wayfarers, and at times the people they supposedly represented were afraid to carry valuables when they went on a journey. But for the most part, the colorful demes were in fact the population's only and quite effective voice in the government.

On many occasions, the demes and the emperor avoided collisions at the last moment. But unfortunately for the demes, they did collide with Emperor Justinian I.

Justinian was about forty-five years old when, in 527, he became emperor. He was very well prepared for the job, for during the nine-year reign of his aged predecessor, his uncle Justin I, he had been chief advisor, and essentially, the power behind the throne. The empire that he inherited had come a long way since the days of Constantine—it had developed its own character and it certainly was prospering—but if one compared it to the Roman Empire of five centuries before, it had lost a great deal, too. Justinian regarded his empire as Rome's successor and longed to regain control of Western Europe. He also worried about the Persians, who still were a serious threat in the East. Moreover, Justinian detected some religious disaffection among his subjects—particularly among Syrians and Egyptians—that he feared would further weaken the empire from within. Even before he inherited the throne, he decided not to deal with problems when they arose but to prevent them from arising in the first place; not to keep the empire from disintegrating, but aggressively to enlarge it and restore the power of the ancient Roman Empire. To do this effectively, he would have to be a strong, aggressive emperor.

Justinian's manner and appearance were somewhat deceiving. He looked like an average man, of medium height, round- and ruddy-faced, and with a tendency to gain weight easily. (He seems to have been on a perpetual diet to keep from getting stocky, and for this reason he was probably the most temperate wine-drinker to sit on the Byzantine throne during those hard-drinking times.) Soft-spoken, gentle, and evidently polite without exception, he was also religious and sternly self-disciplined. There is no record of his ever having lost his temper, even under great strain. He was an insomniac, an industrious worker, and he insisted on remaining approachable and available to listen to the complaints or praise of noblemen and beggars.

But the Emperor Justinian was much more than the reserved, easygoing person he appeared to be. He was firm to the point of stubbornness about his carefully calculated decisions. He was not bound by conventions and was extraordinarily courageous about defying them.

The Byzantines as a people were very superstitious, and Justinian shared many of his contemporaries' beliefs. Like them, he saw no inconsistency in the fact that wizards and sorcerers were believed in with no qualms in Constantinople, but that astrologers were regarded as criminals; if an astrologer was caught within the city limits, he was placed on a camel and driven away by people chasing him and swinging whips at him. The clergy were as superstitious as anyone and retained, with only slight alterations, many of the pagan rituals that were supposed to exorcise demons or cause miraculous cures.

Justinian was quite religious, too. Once, when he was ill, he went directly to the ancient church of Saint Cosmas and Saint Damian on the Golden Horn and prayed to the icons to be healed. He came away healthy and immediately ordered the old church restored and beautified; it became a haven for the sick and dying. Another time the Emperor asserted that an oily substance had flowed from an icon and had cured an ailment from which he had been suffering. He had the robe that he had been wearing soaked in the oil, and it was preserved in the palace as a guaranteed cure for whatever ailed anybody in the court.

Justinian's marriage to Theodora was symbolic of both his willingness to defy conventions and his stubborn courage. One of the most remarkable women of all history, she matched and at times exceeded her husband in wisdom, administrative ability, and determination. Together they provided the empire with its most fascinating—and in several respects, its most able—rule.

Even before Justinian had met her, Theodora had become a well-known personality around Constantinople—the sort of well-known personality that respectable people avoided. Her father probably was the keeper of bears at the Hippodrome, and no one knew who or where her mother was. Having grown up in the coarse environment of the circus and theatre, Theodora was earthy and adventurous, and she made a career in the city as an actress and dancer.

Small, graceful, and very pretty—more than one contemporary account comments that she was in life very much better looking than her official portraits made her appear—Theodora also was charming and quick-witted, with the

The gold medallion above was minted around 535 in Constantinople to honor Emperor Justinian. On one side is a portrait, and on the other, a depiction of the warrior-emperor led by a winged victory.

The speed, danger, and excitement of a chariot race were captured on the third-century Roman mosaic above. The competitors are clothed in team col-

ors, as they were in Constantinople, where such races were held in the Hippodrome and where they became as popular as they had been in ancient Rome.

intelligence and the brashness of a man. Long before her twentieth birthday she had acquired a reputation as a promiscuous woman; the buoyant and open way in which she flaunted her love of life caused endless scandal and gossip.

One day—probably around the year 520—Theodora disappeared from Constantinople. It was said that she went to Libya as the mistress of a governor with whom she later quarreled and parted company. In any case, she seems to have traveled in Africa on her own while improvising ways to earn money for food and travel, finally winding up in Alexandria, at that time a city filled with Christian holy men. There she apparently reformed; and she returned to Constantinople, older, more settled, more sensible, and filled with Christian virtue. She lived quietly and managed to meet Justinian, who was then about forty years old and the advisor to his uncle, Emperor Justin.

Justinian promptly fell in love with Theodora and proposed marriage; but she, aware of her past and his future and the incongruity of the combination, refused. The consul gave her gifts and money, sought her advice on political issues, and even raised her to the rank of patrician, but still she hesitated. Finally, Theodora agreed on the condition that Justin approve the match. To her surprise, the old Emperor, who was captivated by her, agreed in an instant. His wife, however, erupted in opposition, absolutely forbade the marriage, and forced Justin to back down. But soon the Empress died, and Justinian and Theodora immediately planned a wedding. When he discovered a law forbidding the emperor, senators, or any other high official to marry servants, innkeepers' daughters, actresses, and courtesans, Justinian simply had the law canceled. They were married and in 527 assumed the throne together.

Theodora always had been a beautiful and ceremonious hostess with the ability to make her guests think that they were each of tremendous importance to her. But as she settled into the routines of life in the palace, her intelligence and perceptiveness began to work in combination with her natural interest in politics; and she began to assert more than a woman's usual indirect influence in political matters. Now virtuous and stable, she seemed anxious to spend her time competing with men on their own level. From time to time she displayed a streak of the despot as she conferred with her husband's aides; and she used her theatrical talent in combination with her strong will in order to make her points or enact her programs.

Soon Theodora was interfering in everything. She filled

BOTH: DUMBARTON OAKS COLLECTION

Like a bride in ancient Rome, a Byzantine lady wore a ring and marriage belt at her wedding. The examples at left and below differ from Roman counterparts in that the images incised into the gold are Christian. The bust at right generally is supposed to be Theodora, the lovely former dancing girl, who must have worn such jewelry when she married Justinian and became Empress of Byzantium.

CASTELLO SFORZESCO, MILAN: SCALA

the palace and the bureaucracy with her relatives and protégés. She dismissed Church officials on whims and hired others impulsively. When she disagreed with the Emperor's orders, she simply replaced them with her own. And yet, during the twenty-one years of her reign, she saved the throne a number of times for Justinian—for her political instincts were sounder than his. And she was responsible for several progressive welfare programs. (One such program provided wayward girls with assistance in the form of shelter, money, food, and even pretty dresses. She was determined that no young girl in her empire ever would have to live as she had in her unfortunate youth.)

Had it not been for Theodora, Justinian's regime might well have come to an end during the Nika Rebellion of January, 532. Named for the Greek battle cry *nika, nika,* or "conquer, conquer," the rebellion began with a riot of demes and spread to all levels of society.

During the reign of his uncle, Justinian had been re-

Some time after Justinian rebuilt the imperial palace, a series of mosaics depicting pastoral scenes were set into the floor. In the section of that series shown below, an eagle holds sway over a serpent.

garded as an ally of the Blues in the Byzantine government. When he had become Emperor, however, he had tried to appear above partisanship. It was not a particularly good idea. This show of independence did not ingratiate him to the Greens, and it alienated the Blues. Moreover, the people regarded his aloofness from the demes as an indication that the Emperor did not take seriously their representatives' role in the conduct of government, and they resented it.

The first five years of Justinian's rule produced an unusual alliance between the demes and several senators and other government officials who were alarmed at the cavalier fashion in which the Emperor spent the empire's military and monetary resources. At virtually any given time Byzantine armies were off fighting; to pay for the expeditions, the taxation of Byzantine subjects was extraordinarily heavy. At home, meanwhile, Justinian had established a policy of harsh punishment to members of the demes caught robbing or plundering. The demes were dissatisfied with him, and the senators—particularly the older ones, who remembered more moderate leaders—feared that he would bankrupt the empire. The result was an alliance that eventually developed into the bloody Nika Rebellion.

Late in 531 and early the next year the demes in the Hippodrome argued, with increasing regularity, about who was responsible for the financial troubles of the empire. Some blamed military adventures, others blamed the poor management of Justinian's finance minister, John the Cappadocian. One day in the great arena, a fight—not an unusual occurrence—broke out between several Blues and Greens. In accordance with his policy of firmness with the demes, Justinian sent troops to arrest the rioters, and all who had been involved were given stiff punishments.

As repression often does, Justinian's handling of the riot backfired. Instead of providing an object lesson for the demes, he united them: Blues and Greens marched together and were joined by aristocrats and working people in calling for his overthrow. In fact, they contrived to replace him with Hypatius, who was a descendant of an earlier emperor.

During the several days following the Hippodrome riot the insurrection gathered force. Arsonists kept the city in flames, and no member of Justinian's court was safe out of doors. Finally, the rebel leaders decided that the time had come to crown the new emperor, and word spread through the rebels' ranks for all to converge on the Hippodrome.

Justinian himself heard the news and hurried to the arena. Carrying in his hand a gospel to swear upon, the Emperor addressed the crowd and acknowledged its victory. There would be an amnesty for all involved, he said, and a substantial tax reduction. But the mob was too excited and refused to listen to the Emperor. And not far away, in the Forum of Constantine, some of the rebels were preparing to crown Hypatius, escort him to the Hippodrome, and place him in the Emperor's box. Ignored, Justinian hurried out of the arena and back to the imperial palace. As far as he was concerned, the rebellion had been successful: he was ready to leave Constantinople.

But Theodora had other plans. Meeting with Justinian and his loyal generals at the palace, she addressed the men calmly and as an equal. A courtier named Procopius was present and recorded her words:

In my opinion this is no time to admit the maxim that a woman must not act as a man among men; nor, if she fires the courage of the halting, are we to consider whether she does right or no. When matters come to a crisis, we must agree as to the best course to take. My opinion is that, although we may save ourselves by

Their handles decorated with a boar's head motif, this pair of silver spoons reflect not only the wealth of the imperial court at Constantinople, but also the attention paid to lavish details.

flight, it is not to our interest. Every man that sees the light must die, but the man who has once been raised to the height of empire cannot suffer himself to go into exile and survive his dignity. God forbid that I should ever be stripped of this purple [the royal robe], or live a single day on which I am not to be saluted as Mistress. If thou desirest to go, Emperor, nothing prevents thee. There is the sea; there are the steps to the boats. But have a care that when thou leavest here, thou dost not exchange this sweet light for an ignoble death. For my part I like the old saying: the empire is a fine winding sheet.

Inspired and determined, Procopius writes, the imperial party resolved to remain and to retake the power that had been wrested from them. As they planned their strategy, they realized that the rebels were in the process of making a very serious error: they were assembling within the walled Hippodrome. Since there probably were close to eighty thousand of them in a place meant for sixty thousand, the rebels were vulnerable to an attack from without.

Justinian's costly military campaigns in the West restored to the Crown much of the lost territory of the old Roman Empire. The conquests never proved to be very profitable, but they pleased Justinian and his subjects.

While one general mobilized the comparatively few available soldiers, the palace guard, and any other arms-bearing men he could locate, another went to the Hippodrome. There he secretly informed several of the more opportunistic demarchs that Justinian's "army" was en route to the arena and soon would have it encircled. A number of the Blues' demarchs correctly evaluated their own vulnerable situation and either removed their men or decided to fight on Justinian's side.

What followed was a massacre. The improvised army of invaders entered the Hippodrome, and when many of the reconverted Blues inside began attacking their fellow rebels, the assembly was reduced to chaos. Contemporary sources usually place the number of deaths at thirty thousand, and few modern historians dispute that figure.

With Justinian's merciless crushing of the Nika Rebellion, the only democratic element in the Byzantine autocracy disappeared. The Emperor had been reluctant to destroy the demes, but Theodora, who chose not to be destroyed by them, displayed no such reluctance. She prevailed.

His opposition silenced, Justinian resumed his many programs for the glorification of his empire. At Theodora's suggestion, he instituted a new policy of tolerance toward some of the non-Orthodox peoples of the realm—Syrians and Egyptians, for instance. Since Persia represented a greater potential threat to the empire than the barbarians of the West, the Empress reasoned, their best protection in the East was satisfied people who would resist, rather than welcome, invaders. When good relations in the East were established, the Emperor turned the greatest portion of his military attentions to the West. Dominating—though not entirely overpowering—the Vandals in North Africa, the Ostrogoths in Italy, and the Visigoths in southern Spain, Justinian's armies restored the heart of the old Roman Empire to the new.

As though the expenditures of his far-flung military ventures were not enormous, Justinian also undertook a lavish rebuilding of Constantinople. Some of the reconstruction, to be sure, was essential: the fires of the Nika Rebellion had destroyed the entire center of the city. But whether or not there had been a rebellion, it seems likely that the Emperor would have rebuilt the city anyway. He was that sort of ruler: profoundly concerned with all the trappings of power. In his view, the successor to the ancient Roman Empire would have to have a worthy capital.

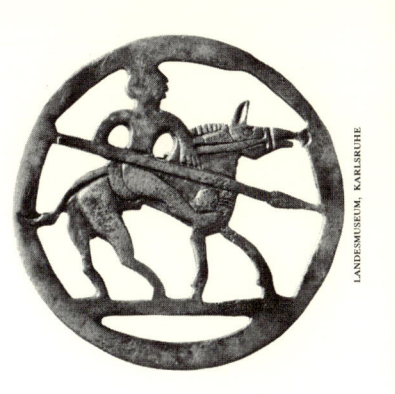

Barbarian warriors, such as the one on the sixth-century Germanic medallion above, tried to encroach upon Justinian's empire.

IVSTINIAN

IV

THE CITY OF JUSTINIAN

Constantine had made Byzantium the capital of the world's greatest empire, but it was Justinian who gave Constantinople the character of a great international city that it would retain for centuries. For seven hundred years the city on the Golden Horn would influence—more than any other metropolis of the time—the evolution of the arts, religion, government, and law in Western civilization. And to an extent not duplicated by any other world capital afterward, Constantinople served to bridge the cultures of East and West.

Justinian undoubtedly regarded the restoration of the heart of the old Roman Empire as his most significant achievement. But that was not the case. The Emperor had re-established some of the frontiers of the ancient realm; but the ancient world did not exist any more; and the new Roman Empire that he so proudly forged did not long survive his death in 565.

What did survive was the culture. No one "founds" a culture, but Justinian's restructuring of his empire's society created an atmosphere and the institutions through which a culture might flourish. In contrast, the West was undergoing a period of constant change, of enormous political and religious upheaval. To the east and south of the Mediterranean the religious disaffection of Justinian's subjects would pave the way, within a century after the Emperor's death, for the success of Mohammed and his new religion of Islam. Within this world of tempestuous change Justinian's empire, and its capital in particular, would provide an imperfect but comparatively stable link between the cultures of East and West, past and future.

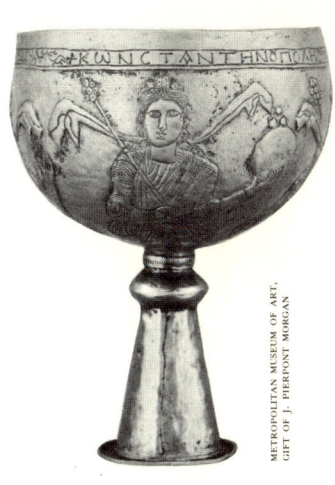

A female personification of Constantinople shares the silver-gilt cup above with representatives of Rome, Cyprus, and Alexandria.

Ravenna, on the Adriatic, was a center of Byzantine culture in Italy. There in the sixth-century Church of Sant' Apollinare Nuovo, the mosaic portrait of Justinian (left) was executed in a distinctively Byzantine style.

The Eastern Christian Empire is most familiarly known as the Byzantine Empire. Its borders stretched and receded often during its seven-hundred-year life, but always its heart and capital were Constantinople. Although it changed a great deal over the years, it remained essentially the city that Justinian bequeathed to his empire.

It was, in the time of Justinian, a city of perhaps six hundred thousand people who called themselves Romans and spoke Greek. As had been characteristic of the population from Constantine's time, the people had a wide variety of ancestry. Some were descendants of Greeks and Romans, of Illyrians, Thracians, Goths, Celts, Cappadocians, or Phrygians. Other arrivals included Egyptian Copts, Syrians, and Armenians. Huns and Germans who served as mercenaries in Justinian's army sometimes settled in the capital permanently. Although the people of Constantinople were inclined to regard those who did not believe in Orthodox Christianity or did not speak Greek as barbarians, they did not entertain any racial prejudices. Intermarriage between persons of different nationalities or races was not unusual and incurred no disapproval, provided

The artisans of Constantinople made splendid use of the precious stones and metals that came to the centrally located port from East and West. At left is a golden bracelet with a floral design; most of its gems are gone, but the Oriental pearls remain. The exquisitely fashioned earrings at right are similar to a pair once worn by Empress Theodora, as the back endsheet of this book indicates.

both parties were Orthodox and spoke Greek. Justinian himself was born in Illyricum, and many of his closest advisors and generals were not of Roman origin.

Life in Constantinople revolved around the government. At the very center of the city's society were the emperor and empress, and they were surrounded by the members of the imperial court—the emperor's council, military leaders, heads of the bureaucracy, senators, and clergy. The court's official ceremonies were cloaked in opulence: such routine matters as the reception of foreign dignitaries and audiences granted by the emperor might become festive pageants marked by colorful processions and lavish banquets. There was also an assortment of religious holidays, which gave the court an excuse to fill its calendar with celebrations.

During these festivals the royal family and their courtiers wore richly decorated tunics and cloaks embroidered with gold thread and ornamented with jewels. Equally lavish crowns, crosses, and scepters were borne in processions. Aristocratic ladies wore precious stones mounted on delicately and elaborately wrought gold pendants and lockets; they carried their cosmetics in exquisitely formed ivory containers and drank from ornate copper and bronze and silver cups. The products on display at the festivals left no doubt that Constantinople was an international city: each celebration was a procession of goods and raw materials from all over the civilized world.

But the grandest display of all was the city itself.

Even though the people of Constantinople were temporarily disenchanted with Justinian after the Nika Rebellion, they were enthusiastic about the program he developed for the rebuilding of the city. Like the Emperor, they craved the monuments and the lavishness that would testify to their position of supremacy in the world.

Money, then, was no object: contributions of cash and goods poured into the building fund. And if people continued to complain about the high taxes, they confined their complaints to comments about military expenditures. The truth was that they would have resented Justinian more if he had not rebuilt his capital.

With his characteristic thoroughness and sense of organization, Justinian first devised an over-all plan for the renewal of Constantinople. He incorporated all of the metropolitan area into his plan—suburbs as well as central city—and while he rebuilt all the stone churches that predated his reign, he enlarged those that were located in particularly depressed or dreary areas. He also rebuilt an old hospital for paupers located between the churches of Hagia Sophia and Saint Eirene near the center of the city. But although he did enlarge it considerably, he did not make it large enough to accommodate the demands of all the poor. Instead, he rebuilt at least three others situated elsewhere in or near the city. On the shores of the Bosporus he constructed a public guest house, where poor people who had journeyed to the capital to do business with the government could lodge, free of charge, in relatively picturesque surroundings.

Justinian dispersed public buildings, forums, and recreation centers throughout the city. The law library was located in the Imperial Basilica near Hagia Sophia. In the vicinity of the Augustaeum, the unofficial "main" forum of the city, the Zeuxippus Baths were restored and opened to the public; thus the city's poor frequented the neighborhood of the major government buildings and church for the purpose of taking baths. In the suburb of Hebdomon, overlooking the Marmara, another public bath was built and with it a handsome colonnade and market place. A shel-

Intricately and delicately fashioned, the details of Hagia Sophia's decoration look more like lacework than rigid stone and bronze. An ornament between arches, above, is encircled by intertwining foliage in stone; an imperial monogram appears several times in the adorning column capital, right. At far right, a more linear, abstract pattern frames a bronze door that may have been imported from Rome for the church.

tered port was constructed in order to stimulate the neighborhood's commercial development. A similar program was enacted for the suburb of Arcadianae. There Justinian created a large seaside park with a marble- and stone-paved court projecting handsomely into the Sea of Marmara. Bronze and marble statuary was transported there from the center of the city and from other parts of the empire, and the suburb, once underpopulated and dull, became one of the busiest and most beautiful areas in the city.

Justinian's major efforts, however, were concentrated on the building and rebuilding of the many churches of Constantinople. In all, at least twenty-five edifices were consecrated anew during his reign, and all—even those that had not been in particularly bad shape before enactment of Justinian's building program—bore the architectural characteristics that revealed that they were, conceptually, the work of the Emperor. Among them, none was grander than the church called Hagia Sophia, which was, for centuries, the symbol of Eastern Orthodoxy and of a strong Byzantine Empire.

Sea of Marmara

1	Column of the Goths	16	Amastrianum
2	Senate	17	Forum of the Ox
3	St. Eirene	18	St. Polyeuktos
4	St. Sophia	19	Aqueduct of Valens
5	Milion Arch	20	The Holy Apostles
6	St. Mary Chalkoprateia	21	Cistern
7	Imperial Basilica and Cistern	22	St. Mary of Blachernae
8	Zeuxippus Baths	23	Cistern
9	House of Justinian	24	Column of Marcian
10	Sts. Sergius and Bacchus	25	Cistern
11	Hippodrome	26	Forum of Arcadius
12	Middle Street	27	Wall of Constantine
13	Senate	28	Wall of Theodosius
14	Forum of Constantine	29	Golden Gate
15	Forum of Theodosius	30	St. John Studius

Though largely speculative, this map of Constantinople during the reign of Justinian reveals something of the vastness of the Emperor's rebuilding program. In fact, the map may underestimate its extent, since it is impossible to know how many of Justinian's buildings have been destroyed. The Pantheonlike building attached to the Amastrianum (16), for example, only recently has been excavated. By dispersing important buildings, the Emperor enlarged the city; the newer, western part of the town was joined to the older east by Middle Street (12), a colonnaded thoroughfare often flanked with peddlers' stalls and canopied bazaars. Water stored in cisterns was transported over an aqueduct (19), which ran into an underground tunnel near the Forum of Theodosius (15). Middle Street ended at the main palace area bounded by the Column of the Goths (1) and the Hippodrome (11). This was the area of old Byzantium; on its edge Justinian built a private palace (9) overlooking the Sea of Marmara. Across the Golden Horn from the many-hilled city was the suburb now known as Galata, which was just beginning to become a residential area during the reign of Justinian.

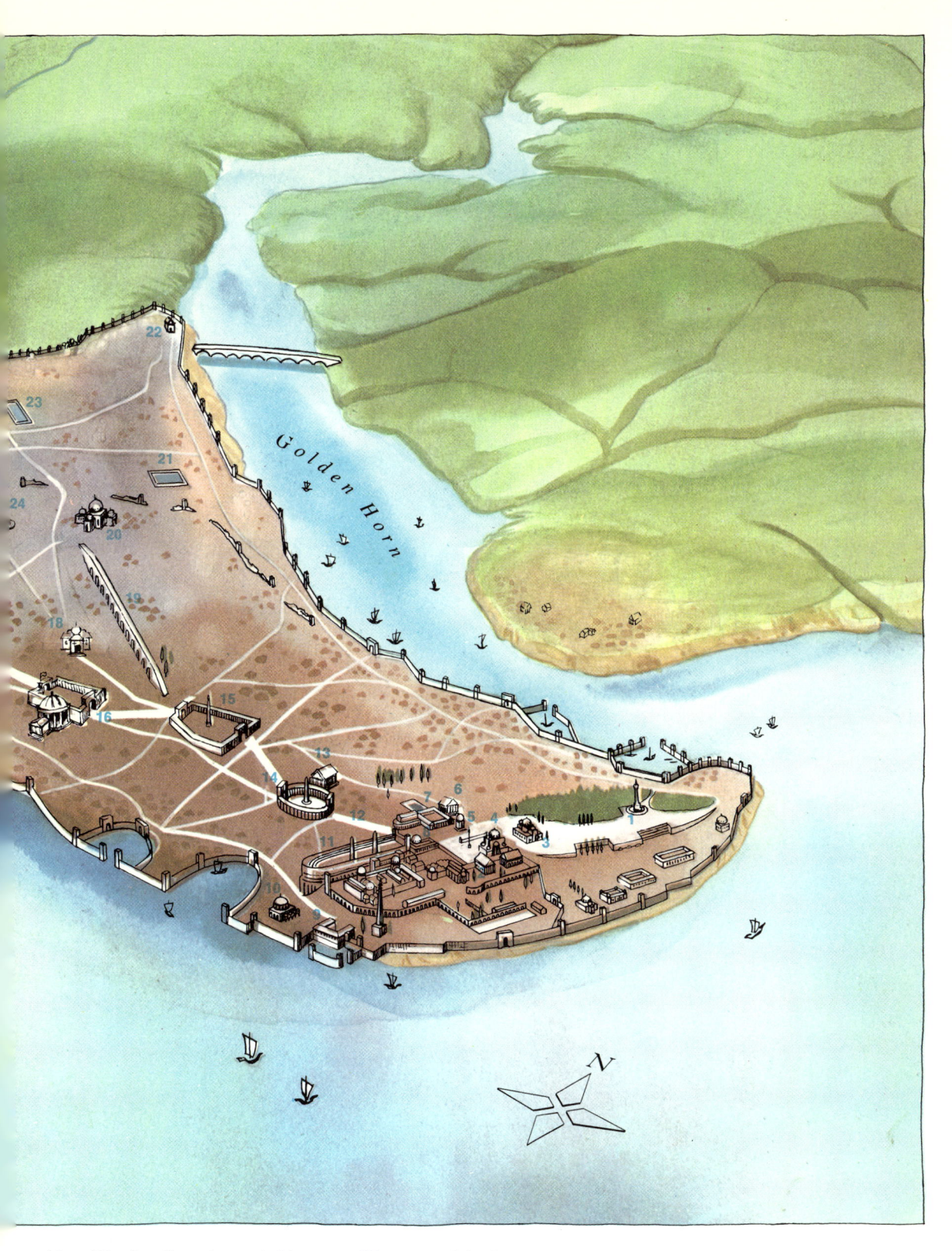

Built according to the cruciform "central plan" favored in Near Eastern architecture, Hagia Sophia is a huge, domed church, vaulted in the manner of some Roman basilicas. No building in Constantinople better demonstrates the familiar assertion that Byzantine art and architecture were essentially a marriage of the styles of East and West. The massiveness and masculinity of the interior— emphasized with great, thick pillars and enormous, even awesome spaciousness—recall the greatest buildings of Rome. And the intricately arranged arches, the rich ornamentation, and the repetitive series of patterned mosaics and inlay clearly are products of Eastern influence.

Hagia Sophia long remained the most glorious edifice in Christendom. Magnificent though the many Gothic cathedrals of Western Europe were, none truly surpassed Hagia Sophia in size, grandeur, or awesomeness. The only Western shrine that might have outshone it—Saint Peter's Basilica in Rome—did not reach its most splendid state until after the fall of Constantinople in 1453. Thereafter, of course, Hagia Sophia was not Hagia Sophia anymore, but Sultan Mehmet's mosque. But for as long as it was a Christian church, Hagia Sophia was supreme. (Today the edifice is neither church nor mosque, but a museum.)

Next to his rebuilding of the city, Justinian's most important contribution to his empire and capital was his decree of 528—issued just six and a half months after he had become Emperor—which established a commission to prepare a new code of laws.

In 438, during the reign of Emperor Theodosius II, centuries of Roman legislation and legal precedents had been compiled in a written code. It was, however, a rather nonselective compilation and contained many obsolete and contradictory laws. Furthermore, a substantial number of new rulings had been made since the publication of Theodosius' Code, and once again the statutes required considerable clarification. In Justinian's time the empire was an all-but-absolute monarchy, with the Senate a figurehead body and the Emperor the sole interpreter and executor of the law. Justinian took this responsibility very seriously: his power to make laws through personal pronouncement had to be matched by his sense of justice; and justice required

Today Hagia Sophia, Justinian's grandest monument, is a museum, but ample evidence of its past as both church and mosque remain. All the mosaics in the interior are Christian; the Arabic roundels are, of course, Islamic.

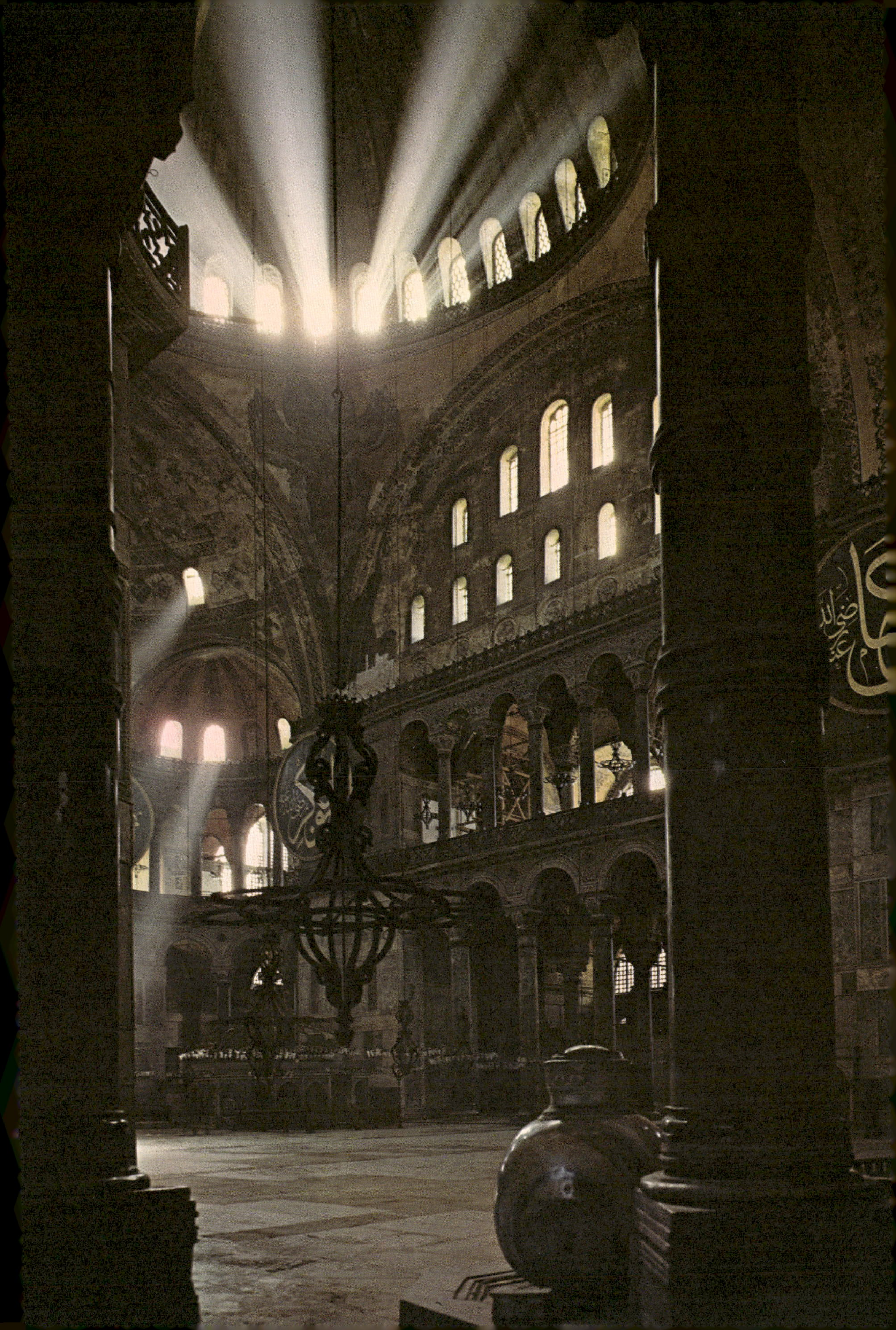

a degree of consistency. By appointing ten distinguished jurists to compile the new codification, Justinian was announcing his intention to execute law on an equal basis to all his subjects.

Essentially, the laws of the empire were Roman. The development of legal codes and restrictions and guarantees probably was Rome's major gift to the evolution of Western civilization. Roman law produced not only a universal definition of human rights, but also ensured a respect for law and the acknowledgment that civilized mankind could survive and prosper only under the law. Without the Code of Justinian, it seems likely that the heritage of Roman law might have been lost.

Basically, Justinian's Code defined the relationship between the individual and the state according to Roman concepts, with certain Christian precepts incorporated. It prescribed the training of lawyers and instructed jurists to consider the spirit as well as the letter of the law in making judgments. It reminded the emperor to regard *philanthropia*—the love of mankind—as the foremost consideration when making new laws. Human rights were more sacred than property rights; the weak were to be protected from the strong. Of course, anyone was permitted to become rich if he could—but not at the expense of someone else. In many cases, courts were instructed to favor the slave over the master, the wife over the husband, the debtor over the creditor, the ward over the guardian.

In practice, however, Justinian's Code did not guarantee equal treatment under the law for all citizens of the empire. Then as now, upper-class citizens more often than not were treated more leniently than were lower-class people for commission of the same crime. Nevertheless, the existence of the Code was a powerful tool for Justinian. It strengthened his hold on the office; it gave an aura of justice to the legal procedures of an autocratic state; and its humanistic qualities restored the people's confidence in the Emperor.

In a way, the Code was the very personification of imperial power. Whenever it was employed to treat people fairly, even in a court of law away from Constantinople, the populace regarded its use as a personal enactment of justice by the Emperor. Its new additions—the "new constitutions," or *novellae*—regulating many points of civil law were drawn up in Greek, rather than traditional Latin, and helped to bridge the gap between the common people and the often unintelligible legal system.

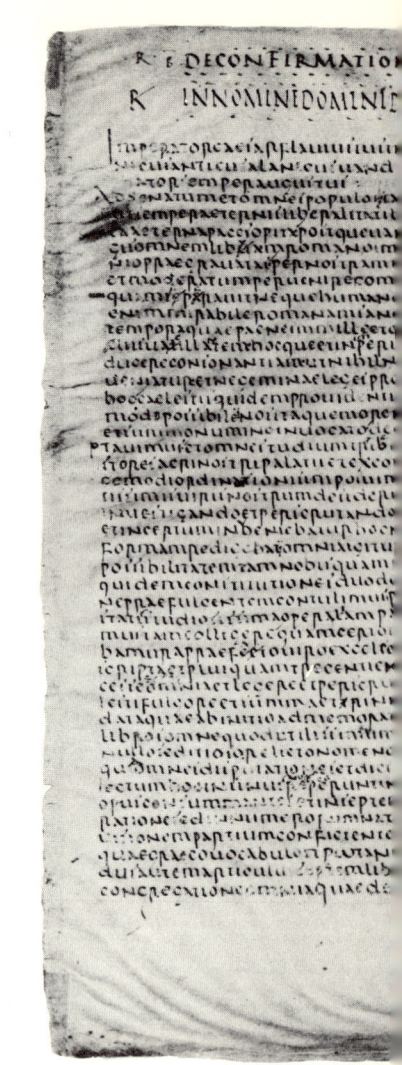

Justinian's Code was a new compilation of Roman statute law formulated at the direction of the Emperor. The somber-looking document above is a page from the introduction, which sums up the virtues of the new Code.

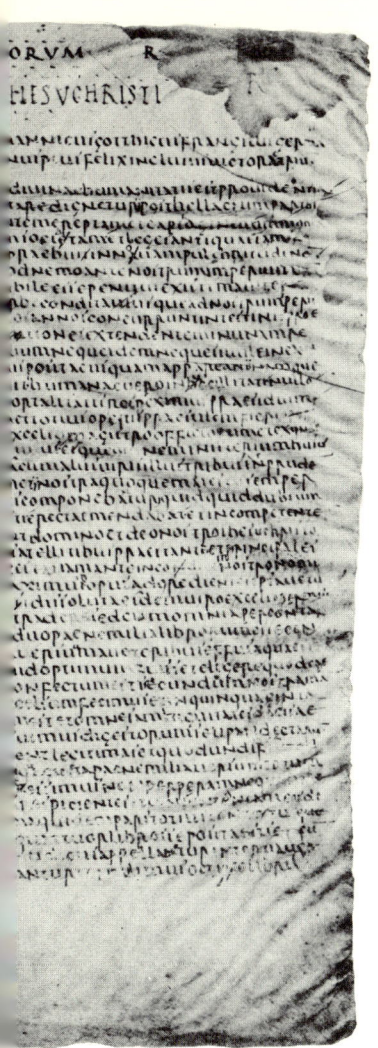

BIBLIOTECA LAURENZIANA, FLORENCE: SCALA

OVERLEAF: *Over the south portal of Hagia Sophia a tenth-century mosaic depicts the Virgin Mary receiving a model of the city from Constantine and a model of the church from Justinian.*

HAGIA SOPHIA, ISTANBUL: PHOTO, ARA GULER

Justinian's Code long outlived Justinian. Indeed, it became the basis for the formation of European law in later centuries. But in his own time the Emperor saw his law supply internal social strength to an empire strong enough to withstand seven of the most eventful and brutal centuries in history.

The spiritual strength of Constantinople was supplied by the Orthodox Church. Religion and citizenship were inseparable in the capital, and the most pedestrian events were accompanied by special sacraments. Specific services celebrated the completion of a new house; certain prayers were said for travelers embarking on a journey; there were sacraments for a mother giving birth and others for the women who assisted at the birth. The calendar was filled with almost daily religious commemorative rites. Services were quite long, celebrated in Greek, and at Hagia Sophia in particular, conducted with great splendor.

Although Constantinople was uniformly Orthodox, the entire empire was not, and this provided Justinian with one of his most vexing problems. The theological issue that divided his realm was not satisfactorily resolved in the Emperor's own time, nor thereafter.

To some extent, the divisive issue had been troubling Christians since the inception of their religion. The question was this: How could the human and divine elements of Christ's life be reconciled? Was Christ man or God?

At Chalcedon in 451 the Fourth General Council of the Church was convened, at which the leading ecclesiastical figures of the empire met to grapple with the issue. The result of the Council was a definition stating that Christ was both God and man—perfect in His Divine nature, perfect in His human one. Thus He was at once above human frailty and capable of human suffering. This sort of definition seemed to appeal to the people of Constantinople, who, like their Greek forebears, retained a love for philosophic speculation and debate.

In Syria and Egypt, however, the notion that Christ could have possessed a divine-and-human duality was unacceptable. More Oriental in their beliefs, and retaining a greater tradition of pre-Christian monotheism, the Syrians and Egyptians preferred a Monophysite theology, in which the divinity of Christ could not be challenged or qualified. Moreover, these subjects of the empire felt that the imposition of the Chalcedon formula was a political intrusion on their traditional beliefs. Monophysite theology became a cause to the people of the Middle East and

ΙΟΥΟΤΙΝΙΑΝΟΟ ΒΑΟΙΛΕΥΟ

ΜΡ

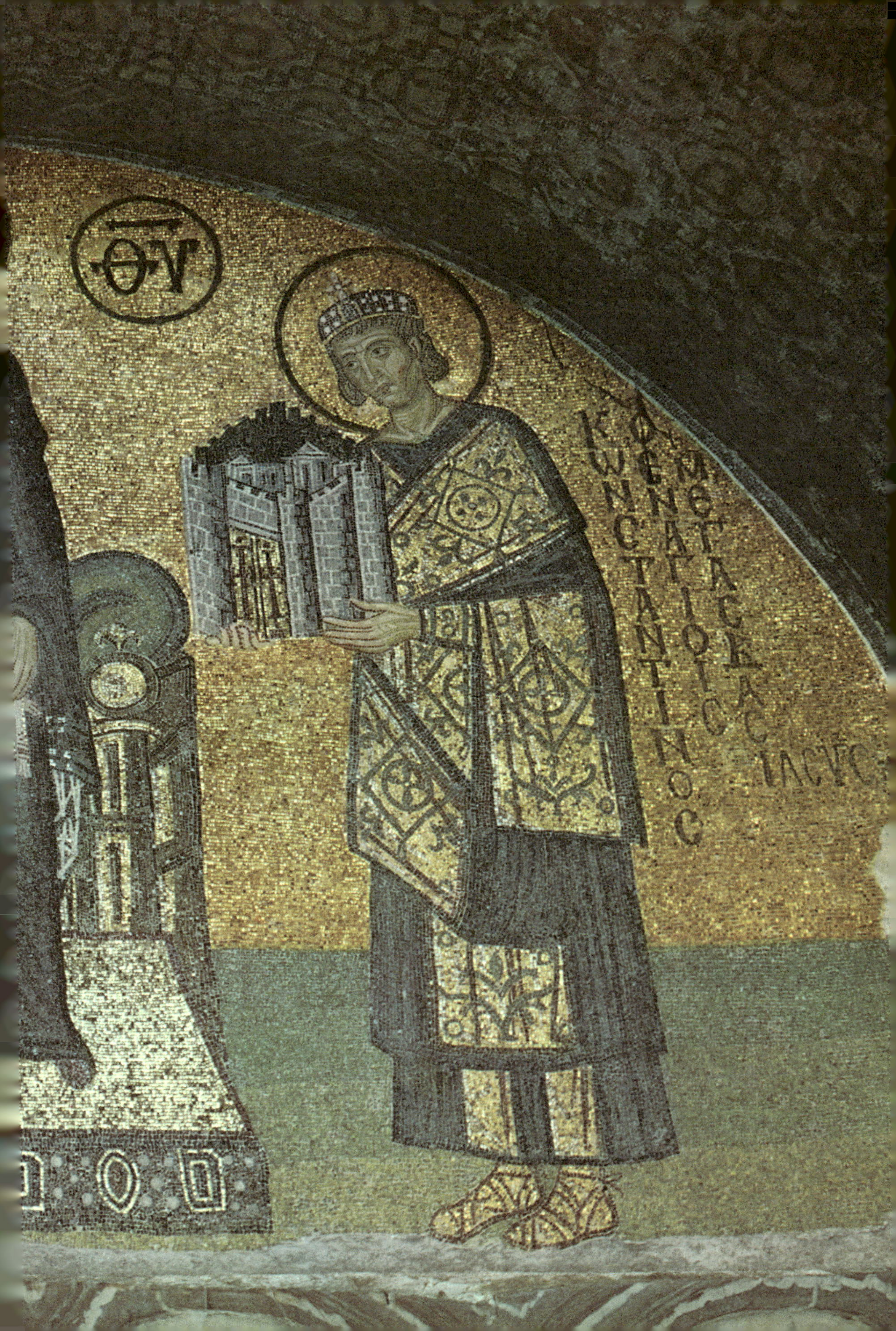
ΘΥ
ΚΩΝCΤΑΝΤΙΝΟC

underlined the many grievances that they had against the government in Constantinople. The problem existed before Justinian, but the Emperor, who was so dedicated to the achievement of unity within his realm, pondered the Monophysites' positions carefully. (One reason for his concern must have been the sympathy that Theodora had for the Monophysite view—a sympathy she apparently had developed during her stay in Alexandria.)

At first Justinian tried a conciliatory policy. After allowing certain Monophysite leaders who had been exiled for their opinions to return to the empire, he invited several of them to Constantinople to meet with some Orthodox priests and try to settle their differences. The conference was fruitless, and Justinian reversed himself, attempting to persecute the alleged heretics: he had several Syrian Monophysites imprisoned, tortured, and executed. But it was known that Theodora actually was harboring a num-

This ivory relief, carved in Constantinople during the sixth or seventh century, is thought to depict the dedication of a church. An emperor, on foot, leads marchers and priests to the site, where an empress greets them.

ber of Monophysites in the palace, and Justinian did not long continue the persecutions. Again he tried negotiation. Although he was severely censured for taking so active a part in theological matters, the Emperor tried and tried again to understand the problem and formulate a solution.

Justinian's involvement with the Monophysites began to worry the Christians of the West, who were afraid that the Emperor would drift too far from the Roman position on theology. In 547 Pope Vigilius was invited to Constantinople from Rome in order to participate in the talks. In truth, Vigilius became a prisoner for seven years, and Justinian alternately pampered and threatened the Pope to get him to yield various theological points. A strong, stubborn man, Vigilius responded by alternately yielding and standing firm.

At one point, Vigilius received word that he was going to be removed from his quarters forcefully and made to agree to all of Justinian's pronouncements. Confident that he would be safe in the sanctuary of a church—where fugitives customarily were not pursued—the Pope and his aide, the Archbishop of Milan, fled to the Church of St. Peter and St. Paul, not far from the imperial palace. When Justinian was told, he decided to ignore the custom and sent soldiers to remove the men. The Pope and the Archbishop clung to the altar, but the soldiers grabbed the Pope by his feet and beard and attempted to pry him loose. Vigilius would not budge. The soldiers pulled harder, but all they accomplished was to pull down the altar, which fell on top of the Pope. Vigilius was not hurt, but the frightened soldiers fled.

When Justinian died, the quarrel between Greek, Roman, and Monophysite Christians still was very much alive. His inability to establish religious unity in the empire to match the legal and geographic unity was his major failure. Nevertheless, his successors did not even attempt to understand the difficulties of religious dissenters. Constantinople and Rome drifted further and further apart, and the Egyptians and Syrians broke off from the empire altogether when the Arabs invaded their lands.

But if Rome and the Middle East drifted away, what was left was a more naturally unified, cohesive Byzantine Empire. Few subsequent leaders even approached the competence of Justinian. Yet—and this was the greatest tribute to his skills—the empire that he left them and its glorious capital were strong enough to prosper and prevail under leaders of sharply varying ability.

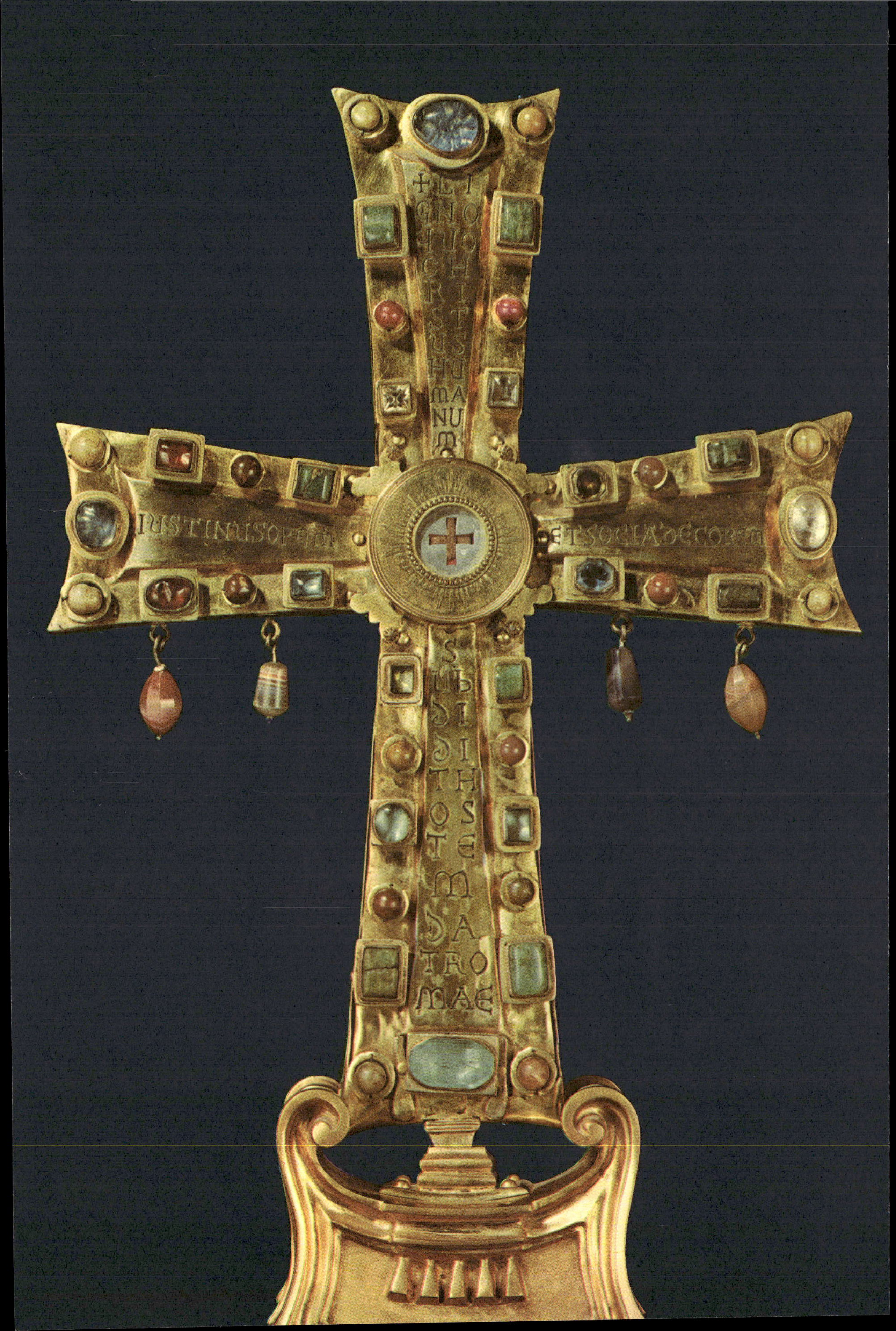
IUSTINUS OPEM
ET SOCIA DECOREM

V

CHRISTIAN CAPITAL

After the death or departure of a particularly strong and active leader—be he caesar, king, or president—a people frequently look forward to a period of calmer, though no less efficient rule. During such periods the entire citizenry has a chance to catch its breath; and more importantly, the gains and changes effected by the former leader can be measured and solidified.

When Justinian died in 565, the people of Constantinople had every reason to believe that they were about to enjoy a quiet spell. The new Emperor, Justinian's nephew Justin II, was a soft-spoken, articulate man who assumed the throne with dignity and a proper respect for protocol. After expressing his devotion to the Orthodox Church in Hagia Sophia, he was crowned at the palace; then he addressed the populace at the Hippodrome. In his speech he issued an apparent clue to his conservatism by promising to settle all of the many debts contracted by his extravagant predecessor.

Justin proved, however, to be anything but conservative. Ill-equipped to possess power, he collapsed under power's weight. While barbarians attacked the empire in the western regions that Justinian had regained, and while Avars and Turks took advantage of the distraction and demanded tribute, Justin quickly went mad. He built a golden chamber in the palace to sit in, as though solitude would make the problems go away. He had himself drawn around the palace in a toy cart. He went into frequent rages, and before long, he was a complete lunatic, incapable of ruling. Once he erected a pillar on which he intended to place a statue of himself. When the pillar, which was inscribed with

Probably modeled after a barbarian captive in Constantinople, the face above appears on a floor mosaic in the imperial palace.

The reliquary cross at left, of silver gilt inlaid with precious stones, was presented to the Pope by Justin II. The gift displays the artistry of Byzantine craftsmen and testifies to the wealth of Constantinople.

83

a list of his virtues, was completed, someone placed a tablet on it that read:

> Build, build aloft the pillar,
>   And raise it vast and high;
> Then mount it and stand upon it;
>   Soar proudly in the sky;
> East, south and north, and westward,
>   Wherever thou shalt gaze,
> Nought shalt thou see but ruins
>   The work of thine own days.

In 574, after nine years of Justin's inept rule, Empress Sophia was prevailed upon to help replace her husband and stop the disintegration of the empire. Sophia simply removed Justin's crown from his head and presented it to Tiberius II. Tiberius was not mad, but his ideas of how to deal with the empire's problems were not much different from those of Justin: instead of facing the problems, he ignored them and tried to crush dissent.

The threats to the boundaries of the empire finally were met when the Emperor Maurice assumed the throne in 582. Despite his competence as a military leader, however, Maurice was an overzealous tyrant, and the people learned to despise him. In 602 the demes incited a revolution in Constantinople. Maurice attempted to flee, but he was appre-

The miniature below, illustrating a chronicle of Byzantine history, depicts an emperor being dragged into the Hippodrome after he was executed by a rival's supporters.

hended and escorted to the circus, where the people demanded his execution.

Under his successor, Phocas, near-anarchy prevailed in Constantinople. Phocas' leadership was less than inspired, wavering between lethargy and despotism, and the factions in the Hippodrome began plotting against him and against each other. During his eight-year reign it was not unusual for the streets to be filled with corpses from one or another of the many insurrections and massacres or from famines that were not effectively combated. Moreover, an army of Persians arrived at Chalcedon and camped there, apparently watching until Constantinople destroyed itself.

In 610 a gallant and popular general, Heraclius, led a fleet of Byzantine ships into the Golden Horn and stepped onto the shore of Constantinople to restore order. His appearance united the people: they drove Phocas from the palace and crowned Heraclius emperor in Hagia Sophia. Because of his reputation as a military leader, the Persians retreated from Chalcedon.

His popularity and military skills notwithstanding, Heraclius almost lost his throne within six years. For in 615 Jerusalem fell to the Persians, and a year later a Persian army returned to Chalcedon. Heraclius negotiated, and when he realized that his negotiations were getting nowhere —and giving the enemy more time to plan the assault on Constantinople—he secretly decided to move his capital to Carthage. A ship laden with supplies en route to Carthage sank, however, and news of his intention became known in Constantinople. Only his popularity prevented a revolution: the people gave him a chance to change his mind—a chance that he took. For good measure, the citizens made the Emperor swear to the patriarch in Hagia Sophia that he never would move the capital of the empire elsewhere.

With that promise made, Heraclius became the most competent emperor of Byzantium since Justinian—principally because he enjoyed the support of the people. After news of his pledge in Hagia Sophia was broadcast, nobles and churchmen sent money and treasure to the palace, and veterans and young men enlisted to drive away the foe. Heraclius mobilized an army and led it through Chalcedon, all across southern Asia Minor, and into the heart of the Persian Empire, driving Persians before him.

But while the Emperor was engaged in the East, some thirty thousand Avars crossed the Balkans into Thrace and advanced to Constantinople. The barbarians camped under the city walls and demanded tribute from the Senate. When

Amusements in the Hippodrome began with the sounding of a horn, such as the one pictured above.

the senators refused, the Avars burned down a number of churches in suburban areas. The invaders must not have known that some troops had remained in the harbor, however; when the Senate sent a small naval force to attack them, the Avars panicked and fled. They periodically returned, but not before the men of Constantinople had rebuilt and strengthened the outer wall.

In 628 Emperor Heraclius returned from his victorious campaign, crossed the Bosporus with his enormous armies, entered the city through the Golden Gate—the ceremonial entrance—and evidently restored joy, pomp, and a sense of majestic power to Constantinople.

The reign of Heraclius, which lasted until 641, was a considerable failure in one respect, a great success in another. It failed because he could not resolve the theological controversy that had been dividing the empire since before Justinian's day. Heraclius probably was the last emperor strong enough, popular enough, and secure enough on his throne to accommodate the demands of his Eastern subjects for religious freedom. That might have stemmed the tide of Islam within the empire—at least temporarily. But Heraclius, though concerned, did not settle the controversy, preferring to leave theological matters to the religious leaders, who could not reach a compromise with Monophysitism. For all intents and purposes the southeastern parts of the Byzantine Empire—Egypt and Syria in particular—thus were lost.

But Heraclius' rule was a remarkable success in that it established an administrative organization that would help the empire survive and even prosper at a time when internal strife, religious controversy, and a succession of inept leaders ought to have ensured the empire's collapse. Heraclius decided to deal with the external threats all around the empire by combining military and civil leadership in the provinces. He had begun the process during his Persian campaign. Each time he had liberated a province, he had placed a general in charge of all of that province's affairs. The general had been instructed to form an army of provincial peasants; and the soldiers had been paid with grants of land within the province.

As a result of Heraclius' arrangement, the Byzantine army became mainly a citizen army, rather than a force of

Mohammed is shown preaching in the Turkish manuscript at right. (In accordance with Moslem law, his face is not depicted.) He gave the dissident Eastern subjects of the Byzantine Empire an alternative to Christianity.

منبر دوزدیلر چونکه خطبه وقتی اولدی رسول
اول منبره چقوب خطبه اوقدی ول خرما

آغچندنا ولان دیرکردنا واز کلدی دخی کلدی
زار بلغین د و کلی خلایق ایشتدی رسول حضرت

Fashioned in Constantinople in the seventh century, the golden bracelet at left includes five coin medallions with portraits of famous men. The Emperor Heraclius is depicted on two coins—at the upper left and bottom right.
DUMBARTON OAKS COLLECTION

undependable foreign mercenaries. Each province, moreover, had its own army—something like a state militia—whose members were fighting to protect their own land. Obviously, this made for more effective military units than the old mercenary army had provided. The system also benefited the empire as a whole. The peasant class was strengthened and became a class of landowners with some economic and political power. And the citizen-soldiers could not be utilized as easily by ambitious officers, bent on a coup, as the mercenaries had been.

The worth of the system established by Heraclius was tested promptly, for his successors were undistinguished men. They dealt inadequately if at all with the Arabs in the East and with the barbarians who crossed Thrace once again and camped at Constantinople's doors. But the citizen armies held their own, and the city was secure.

Constantinople did enjoy one moment of brilliance in the otherwise lackluster period of the late seventh century. In 678 the Arabs, who had been plundering successfully in Asia for years, sailed through the Sea of Marmara and began a siege of the city. Under Emperor Constantine IV the army fought magnificently and turned the infidel invaders back with heavy losses. Representatives from the West soon arrived to render thanks and praise: Constantinople had become the fortress of Europe against the infidels.

Constantine's son, Justinian II, was an erratic leader. An active builder and a reformer of the tax structure, he also was a devout Christian, the first emperor to order the coin of the realm stamped with Christ's image. His government was the first in many years to take on an anti-aristocratic emphasis, and the rights of many formerly unrepresented subjects, such as farmers, not only were restored but also were protected.

But Justinian was in some ways a negligent and incompetent ruler. He was a known extortionist, raising taxes for his building programs and keeping an excess of the money for his own lavish use at his court. He allowed vice and perversion to run rampant at the palace. His two closest advisors were a sadistic eunuch and a vicious monk. An advocate of brutality, indifferent to public opinion, Justinian tried the patience of his subjects for more than a decade; then, finally, their patience ran out. When he tried to banish a popular general, revolution erupted, supported by the aristocrats whom Justinian had opposed. The rebels fought through the palace guard and captured the Emperor, removing his crown and escorting him to the Hippodrome. This time the people did not insist that their dethroned ruler be executed, but as punishment for his crimes, his nose was cut off and his tongue was slit.

Yet ten years later, Justinian II returned from exile to mount the throne again. In a barbaric display of triumph in 705 he took his seat in the Hippodrome, surrounded by the men who had engineered his return. His feet rested on the necks of the two emperors—Leontius and Tiberius III—who had been monarchs in his absence; he later had them beheaded. Justinian ranted and raved for six years, until his subjects no longer could tolerate him. They removed him again from his throne, this time executing him on the spot. Then, to make certain that his kind would reappear no more, the mob entered the Church of Theotokos, where Justinian's little son Tiberius was secluded, tore the child from his attendants, ushered him to the palace, and murdered him.

There were three emperors in the following six years (711–717), but it would be closer to the truth to say that there were none. Sometimes anarchy prevailed; at other times the city was ruled by whichever faction momentarily controlled the emperor, or the treasury, or the armories. But in 716 the Senate and clergy chose as their emperor Leo Isaurian, an adventurer who had proven his worth as a general many times in the East.

A year later the Arabs again arrived at the gates to the city. Their furious siege lasted twelve full months. Emperor Leo III defended the city with patience, skill, and luck. He refused to counterattack before winter; and when winter came, it was, to his good fortune, particularly bitter. After a few weeks he led a raid on the Arabs, who, surprised and freezing, quickly scattered. Before they could regroup, an army of Bulgarians arrived to help Leo and slaughtered many of the enemy. Disease spread among the remaining

Execution or assassination ended the reigns of at least twenty-nine Byzantine emperors. The illustration above shows how the reign of Nicephorus II ended.

Arabs as they made their separate ways back to their ships; later, a series of storms all but destroyed the Arab fleet. Islamic historians have written that of the one hundred eighty thousand men who besieged Constantinople in 717–718, only thirty thousand returned to their homes.

With this auspicious beginning to his rule, Leo III was able to remain on the throne for twenty-four years. He seems to have been an able ruler, but he is remembered more for his ideas than for his ability: Leo was the first of several emperors known as iconoclasts.

In 726 there was a volcanic eruption near the island of Santorin in the empire. For some reason Leo, a Syrian by birth, interpreted the phenomenon as a sign of God's anger. At what was God angry? Leo looked around and saw what he thought was the only possible answer: they, the people of his city, of his empire, were idol-worshipers. To him the

Although they tried regularly, no Arab armies ever penetrated the walls of Constantinople. At right is an unobjective depiction of one Arab-Byzantine encounter, showing the gallant Byzantines defending a city from an army of Arabs who are too frightened to even lift their spears from their shoulders.

eruption was clearly a wrathful warning. He, Leo, obviously was meant to assume the role of God's advocate. He would be both a latter-day Abraham, smasher of idols, and a Moses, bearer of God's law.

The controversy regarding the propriety of depicting lifelike forms in religious art was a very old one, and it was natural that the issue should come to a head in the Byzantine Empire. The subjects of the realm, after all, were descended from peoples with a wide range of beliefs and a number of contradictory traditions. The Greeks and Romans of Classical antiquity had been fond of religious statuary representing their many gods; but they placed more emphasis on depicting and striving to emulate the ideal human form than on actual worshiping of the statues. Many of the pagans, on the other hand, venerated their idols passionately: they made manlike beast-figures and

BIBLIOTECA VATICANA, ROME

The debate over iconoclasm in the Byzantine Empire led to the Second Council of Nicaea in 787. In the manuscript illustration at right, a heretic—so called because he destroyed icons, or images—is prostrate before the churchmen. The crowned figure probably is the official but inactive Emperor, Constantine VI, who actually was only a boy at the time.

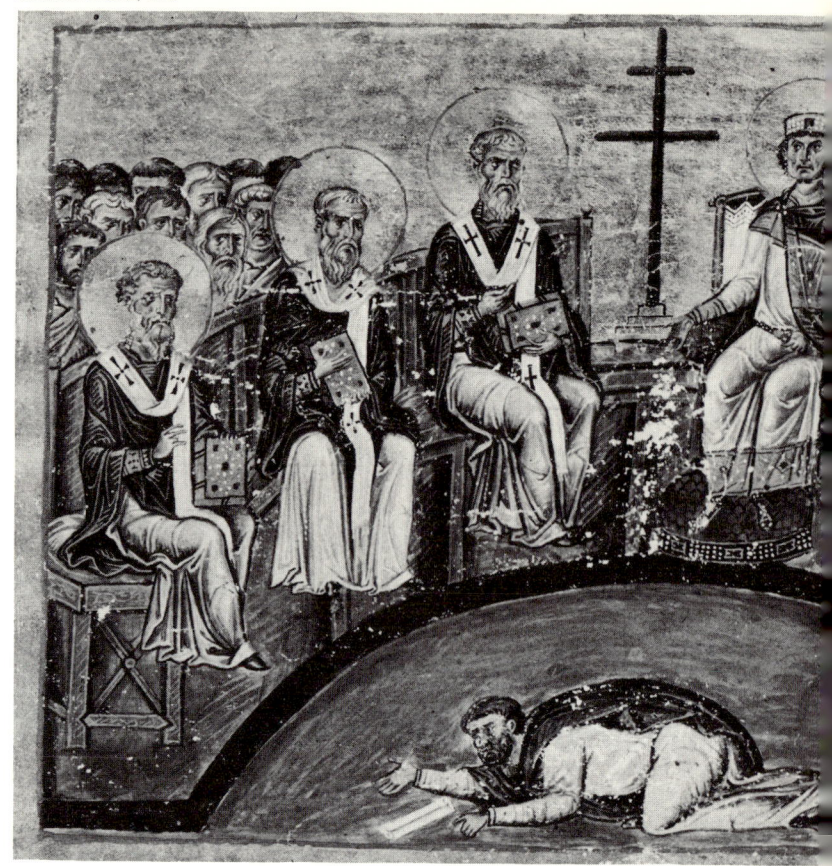

prayed to them, sacrificed to them, and employed them extensively in their rituals. It was this overemphasis on the magical powers of the man-made figure that the early Hebrews had reacted against so strongly. Like some of the monotheistic Egyptians and Babylonians, the Hebrews were more mystical than the pagans and tended to stress individual responsibility in their religious definitions: thus they forbade the fashioning of "graven images." The Jews seldom depicted any human form, because God had created man in His image; therefore, to depict a man was to portray God.

Christianity had many more troublesome and less philosophical problems to occupy it in its early years. The conversions in the third and fourth centuries often were effected without elaborate definition of theology. People who always had made figures continued making figures. When the Church finally took a position around that time, the practice of depicting images already was widespread and was judged acceptable. Always there was a voice in

The dispute over the propriety of depicting holy beings reached a peak when Emperor Leo III (on the coin below left) ordered all icons destroyed. Constantine V (center) was even more vigorously opposed to imagery. Empress Irene (right) relaxed the policy, although it periodically was revived.

ecclesiastical circles opposing imagery, but for a long time it was a minority voice.

Leo was an iconoclast—one who opposed the use of icons, or images of holy beings. He probably was influenced by certain powerful bishops in Constantinople during his reign who were known to be against the widespread use of icons. As a Syrian, Leo may have felt empathy for the beliefs of the Monophysites, who were inclined to be iconoclasts, and for the Arabs, whose Islamic faith forbade depiction of divine beings. In any case, in 730 he declared the many mosaics, reliefs, and paintings in the churches to be idols and ordered them all destroyed. Images were removed from mosaics, walls were whitewashed, coins were collected and melted down, pictures were burned. The population of Constantinople was outraged and occasionally attempted to protect its favorite images. There were executions and massacres, and the destruction continued.

The effects of Leo's order were felt beyond Constantinople. Several provinces revolted, and in Rome Pope Gregory II first protested, then ordered his subjects not to obey the edict, then broke off relations with Constantinople. (It was at this point that the rift between the Roman and Orthodox churches became deep and permanent.) Dissident monks and priests left the empire to settle in Gregory's realm.

But Leo never relented, and his successor, Constantine V, continued his policy with even greater vigor. Not only did he destroy images where he found them, but the new Emperor, who assumed the throne in 741, also declared that anyone who resisted or so much as disagreed with the iconoclasts was flirting with heresy. The greatest center of resistance had been the monasteries, but Constantine took over most of them, murdering many of the brothers, drafting others into the army, and forcing others to marry nuns.

Leo IV, Emperor from 775–780, did not change the unpopular policy. When he died, his son, Constantine VI, was still a young boy, and his widow, the vicious and ambitious

93

In the manuscript illustration above, an icon is being destroyed while two priests try to persuade Leo V to abandon his iconoclast policies. An earlier sect that was opposed to Orthodoxy—and that was regarded as heretical by the Church—were the Arians, who are shown below burning a church.

Irene, ruled the empire. When Constantine came of age and attempted to assume the throne, his mother hired troops to depose him. He was captured, blinded, and exiled.

Irene encouraged the abandonment of the iconoclasts' policies. A pragmatic Athenian, she knew that the controversy bred dissent, and dissent made effective ruling and the assumption of power too difficult. But in 802 her brother-in-law Nicephorus captured and banished the despotic Empress forever, assuming the throne for himself.

Thereafter the empire, and Constantinople in particular, endured a series of brief reigns and bloody revolts under a succession of iconoclastic or anti-iconoclastic ruling families of varying degrees of ability. Fortunately, potential rivals in both East and West were busily engaged at home: in Europe, Charlemagne re-established an independent Western empire, and in the East the Moslems concentrated for a time on erecting in Baghdad an appropriately splendid capital for their young empire.

Just before midcentury, iconoclasm died—but not before its last advocate had caused a wave of terror in Constantinople.

Emperor Theophilus took control in 829. A fanatic iconoclast, he sent for two famous Palestinian brothers, Theodore and Theophanes, who were celebrated pilgrims devoted to icons and who had a considerable following. The Emperor tried to bribe the brothers into denouncing the worship of images. When they refused, he had them flogged, imprisoned, and then exiled. Later he tried kindness and gentle persuasion—to no avail. Theophilus then had the brothers beaten and ordered that twelve insulting verses be branded on their foreheads. The Emperor also sent for a celebrated icon-painter known as Lazarus. Like the Palestinians, the artist would not relent. Theophilus had his hands burned to a crisp.

Still the manufacture of icons continued. A year after Theophilus' death in 843 a council met in Constantinople and revoked forever the doctrine of the iconoclasts. Images again returned to the city.

But the reign of the iconoclasts had been costly. The Roman Church no longer was under the control of Constantinople. The Europe of Charlemagne was about to challenge Byzantium for supremacy in the Christian world. The Moslems in the East were young, strong, and flexing their muscles. Yet, only now was Constantinople, surrounded and challenged, about to become the "Paris of the Middle Ages."

ὁ ἀρ(χάγγελος) Μιχ(αήλ)   ὁ ἀρ(χάγγελος) Γαβριήλ

VI

SEAT OF EMPIRE

In 813 Krum, King of the Bulgars, attacked Thrace and marched all the way to the walls of Constantinople, which he unsuccessfully besieged. Retracing his path along the Thracian peninsula, he laid waste the countryside and overran the city of Adrianople, in the province of Macedonia. He took ten thousand prisoners—men, women, and children—and carried them across the Balkans to the Danube. There, in a colony not far from the land of the Hungarians, Krum resettled the captives.

Almost twenty-five years later, during the reign of Emperor Theophilus, a squadron of Byzantine soldiers made its way north along the Danube in an attempt to subdue the troublesome Bulgars. It reached the colony of forcibly transported Macedonians and offered to escort them back to Constantinople. The Macedonians promptly rebelled against their Bulgar overlords, whose troops they overpowered in four days. Then they boarded the Byzantine ships awaiting them in the river and sailed victoriously back to the capital, where the Emperor thanked them and arranged for their return to Macedonia.

One of the liberated prisoners was a young man of apparently humble origins called Basil. After his return to Macedonia he was appointed to a position of leadership in the provincial army. The reasons for his promotion are not known: probably he had distinguished himself during the rebellion in Bulgaria. Whatever the reason, he soon proved his skill at both military and diplomatic matters.

During the reign of Emperor Michael III, Basil had the good fortune to be in Constantinople at the time of a festival. The events of the celebration included an athletic

Ceremonial welcomes-home were almost commonplace in Constantinople under the far-ranging and warlike Macedonian emperors.

Basil II, one of the Macedonian emperors, stands at the center of the psalter illumination at left. Images of Christ, two archangels, and various saints surround him; groveling at his feet are some of his subject peoples.

The Greek miniatures above depict the rise of Basil the Macedonian. At left, young Basil defeats a famous Bulgar wrestler in competition and wins the admiration of Emperor Michael III. In the center panel, Basil marries Michael's mistress, while Michael discusses the marriage terms with her father; the worried man is Bardas, who knows he is being replaced by Basil as the Emperor's favorite. At right, a man tells Basil that Michael is planning to kill him, but Basil strikes first. Highly questionable, this "self-defense" version of the story obviously is slanted in Basil's behalf.

competition. Because the envoys from Bulgaria had irritated the Emperor by constantly boasting of the achievements of Bulgar athletes, Michael was anxious that his empire be represented by a worthy combatant. His choice was Basil, who fought a Bulgar in the competition and won handily.

Powerful, handsome, and intelligent, Basil became and remained a favorite of the court; he was especially close to Michael. After they fought together in Michael's successful Asia Minor campaign of 859, the two men were practically inseparable. In 865, to help Michael out of a difficult situation, the Macedonian even married the Emperor's mistress, Eudocia Ingerina.

Basil was not, however, second-in-command of the empire. That position was held by a popular soldier-statesman named Bardas, to whom Michael had given the ancient title of *caesar*. When, in the early spring of 866, Bardas embarked on a campaign to recapture Crete from the Arabs, Basil was fearful that the enterprise would further solidify the *caesar's* popularity and strengthen his position as Michael's obvious successor. The Macedonian, who was with the Emperor in Constantinople while Bardas was assembling his troops far from the capital, therefore convinced Michael that Bardas was preparing to seize the crown. On April 21, with the Emperor's knowledge and probably with his approval, Basil ambushed and murdered the *caesar*. As a reward, he received the title of *basileus* and became co-emperor.

Bardas had been the instigator of a number of suspicious programs and he had reshuffled personnel without authorization. But the truth appears to be that he was loyal to the Emperor and mistrustful of Basil. Knowing how close Michael and the Macedonian were, he had had to operate clandestinely. And the secret nature of Bardas' acts had provided Basil with the opportunity to distort them to the Emperor and to make them appear potentially treasonous.

It did not take long, however, for the Emperor to begin to suspect that he had been deceived. The assassination prompted shock, genuine mourning, and anger among the citizens of Constantinople, and many officers and senators expressed their dismay and their suspicions to the Emperor. A revolt in Asia Minor in 867, though nominally aimed at Michael, actually was an expression of resentment toward Basil. Relations between the Emperor and his friend began to cool. And finally, Michael realized that he would have to take action against his friend.

Yet it was Basil who acted first. On September 24, 867, Emperor Michael III was dining at St. Mamas, an imperial residence in a suburb across the Golden Horn. Michael was a hearty drinker, and after dinner he retired to his chamber, heavy-headed from his intemperate consumption of wine. He fell asleep, but before long a band of Armenians led by Basil broke into the Emperor's apartment. Michael had the bad luck to wake—just in time to see swords thrust toward him. As a final indignity to his former benefactor, Basil forbade a funeral: not until the Macedonian himself died eleven years later did Emperor Michael III receive the rites of his faith.

However sordid the details of his elevation, Emperor Basil I, the Macedonian, was a great leader. Most of his military campaigns were successful. He restored the dwindling treasury and handled finances wisely and well. He built and rebuilt the churches and walls of the city. Most importantly, he resurrected, revised, and reapplied the long-neglected code of Justinian as the law of the land. And the dynasty that he established—the Macedonian Dynasty —ruled the empire with authority and competence for almost two centuries.

Under the Macedonians the Byzantine Empire reached a new zenith. It did not extend quite so far east and west as it had under Constantine, but its borders were more realistically defined. The city of Constantinople enjoyed a renaissance of art and literature. With iconoclasm abandoned, the colorful, Orient-influenced Byzantine art appeared again on restored architecture. A reorganized and enlarged University of Constantinople drew intellectuals to the city from all parts of the Middle East. The prestige of the empire and international respect for its power reached a peak, and the court at Constantinople was the most brilliant of the Middle Ages. Commerce flourished, and the city retained its international flavor.

The Macedonians themselves were colorful, often brilliant men, and they set the tone of life in the city. Constantine VII, who officially sat on the throne between 913 and

The beauty of the ivory carving above suits the event that it celebrates: the coronation of Constantine VII in the tenth century. The carving shows Constantine, one of the most sensitive and intelligent of all Byzantine emperors, receiving his crown from Christ.

959, did not really rule the whole time. An infant when his father, Leo VI, died, he was the charge of his uncle Alexander and his mother, Zoe, who were the actual rulers. Alexander died within a year, however, and in 920 Zoe was displaced by a successful general named Romanus. Romanus I and his sons then took over the administration of the empire but allowed the sensitive and likable Constantine to retain the throne in name.

Such a decision on the part of Romanus is testament to the extraordinary nature of Constantine. The historian Edward Gibbon asserted that he "disarmed the jealousy of power." He was an omnivorous reader, a musician, a writer, and a competent artist. He left his successors with remarkably lucid descriptions of life in his time and with evocative analyses of the character and procedures of the imperial court. Romanus was overthrown by his sons in a rebellion of 944. In 945 Constantine overthrew the sons and finally became emperor in fact as well as in name. He ruled competently and compassionately.

Constantine's son, Emperor Romanus II, ruled for just four years before he died. His general married his widow and became Emperor Nicephorus II. A poor administrator

Basil did not know whether he or Michael was actually the father of his wife's son, Leo. But when he became Emperor, Basil imprisoned the youth. In protest, the courtiers, left, staged a sit-in and hunger strike. While their parrot repeats "Ouch, ouch, Sir Leo," the men refuse to dine or budge unless the prisoner is released. Eventually, the Emperor agreed.

and a less than brilliant handler of funds—his ineptness at financial matters led to a devaluation of the currency—Nicephorus was not a popular leader. The palace had to be fortified against an assault by the people, and more than once he was stoned in the streets. He allowed the city to fall into disrepair, and his occasional diplomatic tactlessness vastly broadened the already wide gap between the churches of East and West.

Nevertheless, Nicephorus was an important and in many ways a great Byzantine emperor. A brilliant military strategist with a knack for delegating responsibility to field generals as brilliant as himself, he strengthened the empire wherever he dispatched his troops. He restored northern Syria, Sicily, and Cyprus to the empire, humbled Arabs in the East and Bulgars in the West, recaptured and returned to Christianity the city of Antioch, the seat of an Orthodox Patriarchate. The loss of the city three centuries earlier had been one of Eastern Christianity's saddest events.

The winning of Antioch late in 969 was probably the most notable achievement of the reign of Nicephorus II. Within six weeks, however, he was dead. Joining forces with Empress Theophano and a number of courtiers concerned about the financial troubles during Nicephorus' reign, a young Armenian nobleman, John Tzimisces, who had been the Emperor's commander in the East, murdered the triumphant ruler, whose name meant "victorious." Despite Nicephorus' lack of popularity, his assassination was widely deplored. A contemporary poet, noting the Empress' indispensable role in the conspiracy, composed an appropriate epitaph:

> O Nicephorus, well-named indeed, since thou wast
> Conqueror of all thine enemies, except thy wife.

John Tzimisces became Emperor John I and ruled until 976. Although he was challenged immediately from within his capital—by a faction led by Basil, the son of Romanus II—the new emperor applied himself tirelessly to continuing Nicephorus' valuable policies and mending the damage of his unwise ones. After subduing the rebels at home, he marched into Bulgaria, where his predecessor had been waging a war against the Russians. Under the leadership of Prince Igor of Kiev and his son Svyatoslav, the Russians had become a persistent threat to the power of the Byzantines in the West. In 941 Igor had led a fleet to Constantinople and attacked the city, but the Byzantines had driven his ships away with the dreaded "Greek fire"—

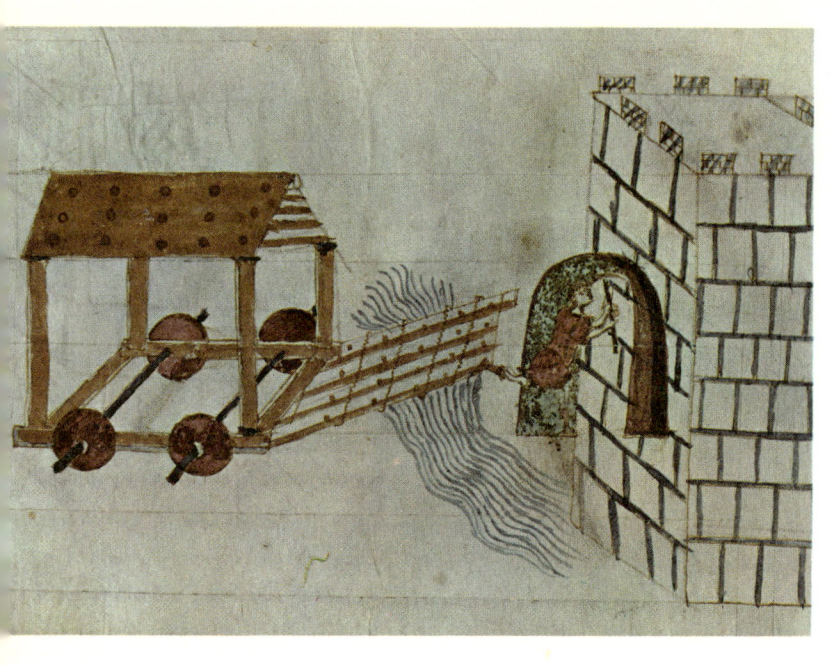

In his Book of Machines of War *the inventive Byzantine military strategist Hero presented his ideas for portable bridges helpful for invading walled cities. For a siege from land of a riverbank town, the bridge at left supplied an arch to protect the invader as he scaled the walls. The movable bridges below were for invasions from the sea; and one was equipped with a battering ram.*

103

BIBLIOTECA NACIONAL, MADRID

A unique weapon in the Byzantine arsenal was a primitive but highly effective flame thrower. In the illustration above, the terrifying "Greek fire" is turned on an enemy during a naval battle.

flames shot from a primitive flame thrower. Three years later the Russians had tried again—by land—but the armies and diplomats of Byzantium had met them at the Danube with tribute, thereby placating the would-be invaders. By the time of John's rise to power, the Russians under Svyatoslav had occupied Bulgaria and Thrace. The year 971 was marked by a series of exceedingly fierce battles, a majority of which were won by John, and by summer's end, the Russians sued for peace and evacuated Bulgaria.

With the western frontiers of the empire no longer threatened, John turned his attention to restoring, as best he could, the damaged relationship between Constantinople and Rome. He did not establish *détente*, but he did manage to avoid further deterioration of the relationship. Finally he turned eastward to continue his predecessor's efforts to secure the borders of the empire against the thriving Arabs. What John I undertook he as often as not achieved, and he developed into a great emperor. He died after only eight years on the throne, probably a victim of poisoning.

John's stern, autocratic, sometimes cruel but often benevolent successor was Basil II, who became emperor in 976 and reigned for nearly fifty years. During his reign the empire extended from the Danube to Crete and from southern Italy to Syria, and the treasury was so well-stocked that new vaults had to be built in Constantinople to contain all the gold and tribute from abroad. But after his death in 1025 there was no strong leader to take over. The aristocracy, military, and bureaucracy struggled to control the succession of weak emperors who sat on the throne. The unity of the empire dissolved as civil disorder became commonplace in Constantinople and anarchy prevailed in the provinces.

In 1081 the Byzantine throne was being bitterly contested. The city's dissident elements quarreled and strove to undermine one another. But this domestic friction ceased when an external peril suddenly appeared across the Bosporus. There, at the tip of Anatolia, an army was pitching tents. It was the Seljuk Turks.

The Seljuks were descended from several Mongolian tribes that had been wandering on the edge of Persian civilization for centuries. Originally, they had been nature-worshipers but had embraced Islam earlier in the tenth century when they had come in contact with Arabs. According to an old legend, Mohammed himself had told his followers: "Learn the language of the Turks, for they are destined to rule long."

In 1071 the Seljuks, noting that the Byzantine forces at the eastern outposts of the empire were dwindling (many of the troops were recalled to deal with disorders in Constantinople or in other provinces), had advanced into Anatolia. The Emperor Romanus IV had led a force against them but had been defeated. During the following decade the Turks had continued their penetration of the peninsula, and now, in 1081, they arrived at the tip.

The crisis brought to the throne in Constantinople the warrior Alexius I, scion of the House of Comneni, a power-

Descendants of Mongolians and converts to Islam, the Seljuk Turks were skillful warriors and constant threats to Constantinople. At left, a Seljuk prince is depicted on a Persian bowl.

The medieval French illustration above depicts the scaling of Jerusalem's walls during the First Crusade. Scenes from the Passion of Christ are shown to point up the holiness of the city.

ful feudal family. Gathering all the forces at his command, Alexius surprised the Turks and drove them deep into Anatolia. He could not continue the campaign, however, because at the same time, a large Norman force attacked the empire in the West. The Emperor restored some of the western regions and dealt with a Patzinak siege of Constantinople in 1091. (The Patzinaks were a tribe of nomads who plundered the Russian steppes and the Balkans in the eleventh century.) Then he prepared to resume his thrust into Anatolia.

Alexius' plans were thwarted, however, when advance elements of the First Crusade crossed Thrace and paused at the gates of Constantinople. The Emperor had asked the West for help some years earlier, with no success. But when the city of Jerusalem fell into Moslem hands in 1077, Pope Urban II convinced the rulers of Europe to answer Alexius' plea. Crying "God wills it!" the Europeans launched the Crusades and became defenders of Christianity.

In 1096 a contingent of Crusaders reached Constantinople, but they were not allowed to enter. Alexius met with their leaders and offered to support them, provided that all recovered Byzantine lands be restored to him. They agreed, and landing in Anatolia, began brutalizing, butchering, and looting without regard to race, creed, or political conviction; the Greek Christian peasants in the Anatolian villages were the first victims. When the Crusaders finally did engage the Turks, the Seljuks had little trouble driving them back to the Sea of Marmara and killing most of them. The survivors were given sanctuary in Constantinople, but they proved so troublesome there that the Emperor permitted them to remain only after they surrendered their weapons.

When more Crusaders arrived in December, Alexius demanded that their leader, Godfrey of Bouillon, swear allegiance only to him. At first Godfrey refused, and Alexius would not let him or his men into Constantinople. When the French duke ordered his troops to camp outside the city, Alexius stopped their supply of food. At one point, Godfrey ordered his men to attack the city, but they were repulsed at the walls. Finally, the Westerner and most of his allies consented to the oath, passed through Constantinople, and were ferried across the Bosporus. Still more Crusaders arrived and joined their brethren in Anatolia. With Byzantine help, they cleared most of Asia Minor—but not the important central plain—of Turks, whom they drove back, all the way to Antioch, and then to Jerusalem. In 1099 the

OVERLEAF: *As armies from the Western Christian world marched toward the Holy Land in their several crusades, Constantinople —which lay directly in their path —suffered terribly from their greed. Note that the city has been turned sideways and placed on the wrong side of the Bosporus Strait on the map. Actually, Constantinople is on the west bank, and the apex of its triangular shape points eastward.*

107

ENGLAND
London
Hastings
FLANDERS
Seine
Meuse
Paris
Vezelay
Clermont
FRANCE
Rhône
Aigues-Mortes
Marseille
Genoa
Pisa

THE HOLY ROMAN EMPIRE
Rhine
Oder
Elbe
Vistula
POLAND
Danube
Vienna
Budapest
Venice
HUNGARY
Belgrade
Zara
SERBI

CORSICA
Rome
Naples
TYRRHENIAN SEA
SARDINIA
ADRIATIC SEA
NORMAN KINGDOM OF SICILY
SICILY
IONIAN SEA

Tunis

MEDITERRANEAN

○ CITIES
✗ BATTLES AND SIEGES
SCALE 0 50 100 150 Miles

THE CRUSADES

EUROPE AND THE HOLY LAND ABOUT 1140

The fifteenth-century French miniature at left was supposed to depict the Crusaders' ships anchored near Constantinople. The erroneous location of the city—on a hill in the distance rather than at the shore—makes it seem probable that the artist never was there.

Holy City finally was restored to Christian rule. East and West had achieved the triumph together, but their relations had not been improved. Indeed, the schism grew in the years to come.

Throughout the twelfth century the Byzantine Empire dwindled, and the best that an emperor in the capital could do was to slow the disintegration as much as possible. Most ominous of all for the Byzantines was the ever-growing power of Western Europe. When Pope Innocent III encouraged the lords of the Holy Roman Empire to embark on the Fourth Crusade in 1199, the interests of the Byzantines were ignored. It was as though the West had ceased to regard the Byzantines as Christians.

At first the Crusaders planned to sail directly to the Holy Land (which again had fallen into Moslem hands), bypassing Constantinople altogether. Once that decision was made, the Western leaders quite naturally turned to the Republic of Venice to forge an alliance. As the world's foremost sea power at the time, Venice could furnish the Crusaders with transportation.

Enrico Dandolo, Doge of Venice, agreed to supply the Crusaders with ships "for the love of God"—and for a substantial fee. He also insisted that Venice be rewarded for its devotion to the holy cause with half of all the land and loot that the Fourth Crusade yielded.

When the Crusaders assembled on an island off Venice, the Venetians suddenly insisted on payment in advance. No one could produce enough funds, but the Venetians proposed a deal: they would provide the ships if the Crusaders first would retake the port city of Zara on the Adriatic, which was then the property of the king of Hungary. The Franks had no choice but to agree, if the Crusade was to go on, and in November, 1202, the expedition sailed for Zara. The assault took only five days. Zara was returned to Venice, and the Crusaders looted it dry. If any doubts had existed about the Venetians' motives, they now were dispelled. Venice was not interested in the Holy Land or in holy causes. It wanted to secure control of the waters north of the Mediterranean. And it probably wanted Constantinople.

The Eastern Empire was ruled at the time by Alexius III. His younger cousin, who also had sought the throne and who also was named Alexius, had become acquainted with the Marquis Boniface of Montferrat, one of the leaders of the Western European Crusaders. After the Venetians and their allies had taken Zara, the Emperor's rival arrived and invited the troops there to assist him in recovering the Byzantine throne. In exchange, he would place the Eastern Empire and throne under the religious domination of Rome. He promised, in addition, to contribute two hundred thousand silver marks to the Crusades and eventually to furnish ten thousand troops. The offer was made even more attractive by the riches of Constantinople itself. No city on earth promised greater rewards to looters and plunderers. The Pope was not enthusiastic: he sincerely had hoped that this Crusade would restore the Holy Land to Christian domination, and he had been infuriated by the attack on the Christian city of Zara. (He also had excommunicated the Crusaders.) Nevertheless, young Alexius' offer, the approval of Boniface, and the vigorous support of the Venetians—who probably had had this in mind the whole time—outweighed the Pope's objections, and the noncrusading Crusaders sailed for Constantinople.

There was nothing subtle in the attitude of the Crusaders toward their fellow Christians. The Crusaders regarded the Byzantines as their enemy and Constantinople as a fortress to be captured and stripped of loot. One of the participants in the Christian assault on the Christian city was a Frenchman, Geoffrey de Villehardouin, Chief of Staff to the Count of Champagne. Villehardouin kept a detailed chronicle of the events he witnessed. As far as he was con-

Because they controlled so much of the West's currency, the Venetians virtually controlled the expensive Fourth Crusade. The larger coin was minted in Venice; the smaller one was minted for the use of the Crusaders.

cerned, the Crusaders were noble and just, and his report condemns the Byzantines, whom he calls Greeks, while praising the Westerners. Nevertheless, any detached modern reader can perceive the reality of the situation.

The fleet landed in Galata, the suburb of Constantinople beyond the Golden Horn, in June, 1203. Across the famous inlet a chain had been extended. After a bloody battle the Europeans managed to seize the tower on Galata to which one end of the chain was fastened; the chain was released, and the Venetian ships sailed into the Golden Horn and filled the harbor of Constantinople.

The assault began from land and sea. According to Villehardouin's description, the Crusaders always were brave, the Greeks alternately strong and cowardly, depending on the needs of the narration:

... [The] attack was stiff and good and fierce. By main strength certain knights and two sergeants got up the ladders and made themselves masters of the wall; and at least fifteen got upon the wall, and fought there, hand to hand, with axes and swords, and those within redoubled their efforts, and cast them out in very ugly sort, keeping two as prisoners. . . .

Meanwhile the Doge of Venice had not forgotten to do his part, but had ranged his ships and transports and vessels in line, and that line was well three crossbow-shots in length; and the Venetians began to draw near to the part of the shore that lay under the walls and the towers. Then might you have seen the mangonels shooting from the ships and transports, and the crossbow bolts flying, and the bows letting fly their arrows deftly and well; and those within defending the walls and towers very fiercely; and the ladders on the ships coming so near that in many places swords and lances crossed; and the tumult and noise were so great that it seemed as if the very earth and sea were melting together. . . .

Now may you hear of a strange deed of prowess; for the Doge of Venice, who was an old man, and saw naught (seeing he was blind), stood, fully armed, on the prow of his galley, and had the standard of St. Mark before him; and he cried to his people to put him on land, or else that he would do justice upon their bodies with his hands. And so they did, for the galley was run aground, and they leapt therefrom, and bore the standard of St. Mark before him on to the land.

And when the Venetians saw the standard of St. Mark on land, and the galley of their lord touching ground before them, each held himself for shamed, and they all gat to the land; and those in the transports leapt forth, and landed; and those in the big ships got into barges, and made for the shore, each and all as best they could.

Executed in the nineteenth century by a French artist, Eugène Delacroix, the painting above depicts the ravaging of Constantinople in 1204 at the hands of the Crusaders commanded by Baldwin of Flanders.

During the battle the Byzantine defense was magnificent and might have succeeded, except that after two weeks Emperor Alexius III lost his nerve. Packing as much treasure as he could carry, he abdicated and departed through a gate in the land walls. The Byzantine soldiers then abandoned the defense, took Alexius III's blind brother, Isaac (young Alexius' father), from prison and placed him on the throne. Then they opened the gates to the city, and the Europeans entered. Young Alexius arrived and was crowned co-emperor, Alexius IV. To help the father and son secure their rule, the Crusaders agreed to remain until the spring.

The people of Constantinople resented their new emperors, resented dealings with the hated Latins, resented the presence of the Crusaders. The increasingly tense situation was made worse by the fact that the Europeans were getting impatient to see the money that Alexius had promised them. When he persistently delayed, the Western leaders grew more lax in their support. In late winter a general strike brought commerce to a halt. Arsonists set fire to government buildings. Finally a group of Greek aristocrats seized the palace in February, strangled Alexius IV, reimprisoned Isaac (who died a few days later, probably of poi-

After the rape of 1204 the Crusaders stripped Constantinople of many prized possessions—including the quartet of bronze horses below, which still stand before Venice's church of San Marco.

The silver gilt and sardonyx cup above is one of the thirty-two existing chalices that the Venetians took from Constantinople. Another stolen treasure is the gold and enamel book cover, right, adorned with a portrait of Michael the Archangel and plaques with likenesses of the saints.

son), and installed a nobleman, Mourtzuphlos, as emperor.

The people then turned their fury on the Crusaders. As a result, the Western leaders inside the city ordered the huge army stationed in Galata, Chalcedon, and the other suburbs to attack the city. To defend the walls now was almost impossible for the Byzantines because there were so many of the enemy already within the city. Mourtzuphlos, like Alexius III, fled. Now the city belonged to the troops who re-entered it virtually unopposed.

The Crusaders, who had forgotten the reason for the Crusades, butchered and burned and plundered. Private homes in all parts of the city were set afire, and public buildings were stripped of their decorations. Men were killed on the spot, women were raped, young people were stored in a church to be sold as slaves. Nothing of the slightest worth was left to the population—even the clothing of the peasantry was ripped from their backs. Soldiers are said to have escorted a prostitute into Hagia Sophia, placed her on the throne of the Patriarch, and sung lewd songs while they destroyed icons, ripped down mosaics, burned holy books, and got drunk from wine poured into sacred vessels. As Villehardouin described it:

The booty gained was so great that none could tell you the end of it: gold and silver, and vessels and precious stones, and samite, and cloth of silk, and robes . . . , and ermine, and every choicest thing found upon the earth. . . . never, since the world was created, had so much booty been won in any city.

Every one took quarters where he pleased, and of lodgings there was no stint. So the host of the pilgrims and of the Venetians found quarters, and greatly did they rejoice and give thanks because of the victory God had vouchsafed to them—for those who before had been poor were now in wealth and luxury. . . .

Then was it proclaimed . . . that all the booty should be collected and brought together, as had been covenanted under oath and pain of excommunication. Three churches were appointed for the receiving of the spoils, and guards were set to have them in charge, both Franks and Venetians, the most upright that could be found.

Then each began to bring in such booty as he had taken, and to collect it together. And some brought in loyally, and some in evil sort, because covetousness, which is the root of all evil, let and hindered them. So from that time forth the covetous began to keep things back, and our Lord began to love them less. Ah God! how loyally they had borne themselves up to now! And well had the Lord God shown them that in all things He was ready to honor and exalt them above all people. But full oft do the good suffer for the sins of the wicked.

When the tumult died down, Baldwin, Count of Flanders, was proclaimed emperor of the Latin Empire. It did not amount to much, because Venice claimed—and was given—three eighths of Constantinople, plus a number of Byzantine cities and islands in the Aegean. Boniface received Macedonia and Thessalonica. The booty was divided and the Crusaders went home happy.

Dispersed in the Balkans, throughout Thrace, and in Asia Minor, groups of displaced Byzantines very slowly, and very remarkably, began to retake their lands. One party retook Adrianople and then engineered a successful rebellion in Thessalonica. Another group in northwest Asia Minor established a government in exile and prepared for the retaking of Constantinople. So determined were the Byzantines, and so impressive were their efforts to remain together as a people with a common law, that they began

The Comneni and Palaeologi families, which dominated Constantinople for several centuries, often intermarried. Forebears of Constantine XI, the last Byzantine emperor, were Constantine Comnenos, above, and his wife, Euphrosyne Palaeologina, opposite.

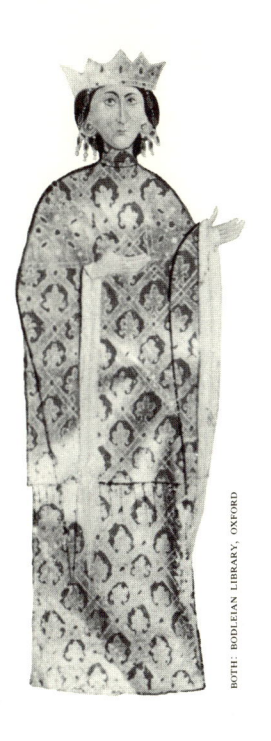

to attract the attention and friendship of some powerful states. In 1261 the Genoese, competitors of the Venetians, signed a treaty of friendship with Michael Palaeologus, who hoped to retake the old capital.

Venetian sea power was formidable, and the dispersed Byzantines had little of their own to counter it. Thus, Emperor Michael VIII agreed to a number of alliances in order to prepare for the recapture of Constantinople. Treaties with the Mongols and Bulgarians were achieved to fortify the western borders; an agreement with a Turkish sultan helped strengthen the Byzantine positions in the east, and the Genoese alliance provided the naval support that was needed so desperately. All of these agreements were very costly—the Genoese, for example, were to be given free access to many of the ports of the Straits and the Black Sea. But without this support, Michael would be unable to capture the lost city—or so he thought.

Actually, Constantinople was recaptured almost by accident. The Byzantine commander Alexius Strategopulus was sent by Michael to keep watch over the Bulgarian frontier. Alexius chose a site near Constantinople to assemble his troops. Arriving there, the commander found, to his surprise, that the city was virtually unprotected: the Venetian fleet had departed with most of the city's troops to besiege an island in the Black Sea. Almost unresisted, the Byzantine forces marched into the city. The Eastern Empire, with Constantinople as its capital, was restored.

But there really was very little left. There were no government institutions, no treasury, no strong army. Flanked by the unsympathetic Latins to the west and the powerful Ottoman Turks to the east, weakened by the alliances that they had formed, the Byzantines knew that they were living on borrowed time, and they tried to make the best of it. The schools flourished briefly; the arts enjoyed a fruitful period. Visitors still were impressed by the city.

The last emperor had the same name as the first: Constantine. He died in 1453 while bravely defending his city from the Ottoman Turks, led by their brilliant young Sultan, Mehmet the Conqueror.

But the truth is that the Turks only finished what was started in 1204, when Constantinople was stripped and violated and humiliated and befouled for no reason but greed. The city never recovered from that. The real assassins of the first great Christian city were not the hated infidel Turks. The real assassins were Christians. They were Cain killing Abel.

PORTRAIT GALLERY, TOPKAPI PALACE MUSEUM, ISTANBUL: SKIRA

VII

CITY OF THE SULTANS

In the summer of 1453 the great city on the Golden Horn was barren and exhausted. The troops of Mehmet the Conqueror had looted all that was there to be looted; they had secured their prisoners for transport to the slave markets of the East; and they were waiting to go home. In the daytime, inactivity made the moist, hot air seem quieter and more oppressive. At night the north wind, Boreas, came down from the hills and whirled aimlessly, lifelessly within the battered walls, only occasionally whipping litter against the broken sides of empty buildings. Victory's euphoria dissolved into homesickness and impatience, for the conquerors were bored.

This was no prize for Mehmet. He had directed the energies of his life to the taking of Constantinople; he had not given much thought to the life of the city after the siege. But the decay that he saw enveloping his informally renamed İstanbul (which means simply "in the city" in Greek) was not, he realized, a fitting sequel to the glorious and successful conquest.

Therefore, he sent the soldiers home, after inviting all who sought a new life to stay. Then he sent word to all parts of his realm that whoever might wish to settle in the new Moslem city would be given a home with a garden and vineyard as a gift of the Sultan. Despite his generosity, however, there was no substantial inflow. Mehmet began to build new mosques, homes, and public buildings and to convert eight of the finest churches in the city into mosques; but labor was scarce, and progress was so slow that he began to grow impatient. He invited Greeks and other Christians to İstanbul and promised them an extraordinary

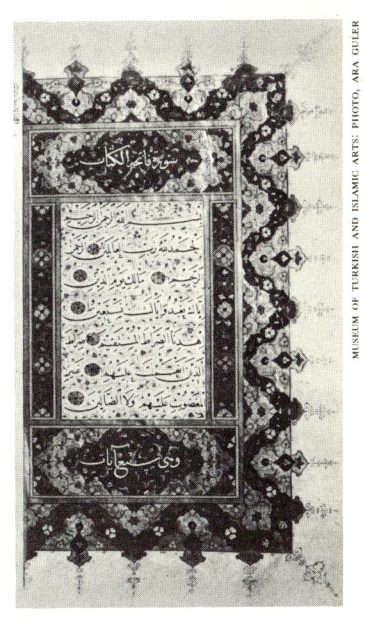

This lovely copy of the Koran—the Moslem holy book—was made for Sultan Bayazid II in 1484.

Though known as The Conqueror, Mehmet was eager to be recognized also for his more sensitive virtues. Accordingly, the portrait by Sinan Bey, left, pictures the contemplative Sultan enjoying the bouquet of a rose.

degree of autonomy. But when only a few Christians came, he extended the invitation to Jews and pagans. Still the city remained underpopulated, and the Sultan ordered many thousands of Greek families to be moved to İstanbul, whether they wanted to come or not.

Western history has not been kind to the Turks. Relations between Christian and Islamic peoples often have been strained, and the imperialistic designs of many European kings and leaders have been disguised under the false name of religion—"cleansing" the Middle East of the "Infidels" too frequently has actually meant securing a commercial gateway to the Orient.

But the Christians of the fifteenth century who found themselves subjects of the Sultan Mehmet and his successors often discovered that their new rulers were, if not better

The floral motif popular in the Moslem world was woven into Sultan Mehmet's handsome velvet caftan, left. In the Persian manuscript illustration opposite, artisans work with tiles to decorate a mosque; here also the floral pattern is prevalent.

COURTESY OF JOHNS HOPKINS UNIVERSITY, JOHN WORK GARRETT LIBRARY, BALTIMORE

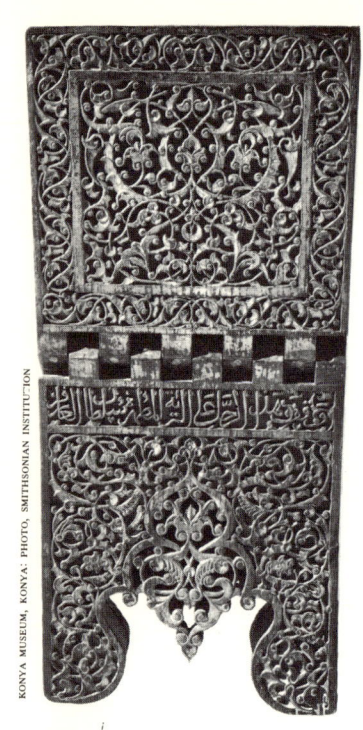

Turkish students often carried foldable stands on which to place their Korans while studying. The richly carved walnut stand above must have had a wealthy owner.

than their former overlords, certainly no worse. The Greeks, for example, virtually were enslaved under the Turks, and yet many of them—the peasants in particular—quickly learned that the Moslem was a better master than the Venetians had been. True, the Moslems regarded their Christian subjects as beneath contempt and compelled them to live in ghettos. But they did allow the Christians to preserve their own language and run their own communities. This amounted to a measure of autonomy that the Roman Catholics seldom had awarded the Orthodox.

With characteristic shrewdness, Mehmet realized that a benevolent if not precisely enlightened policy toward his Greek Orthodox subjects was wiser than a harsh one. Were he to try to wipe out the Christians of İstanbul, he very well might help to close the breach between Roman and Eastern Christians that had been so valuable to Islam. Thus, as he ordered Christians to populate parts of the city, he also installed a patriarch, through whom the Greek Church exercised judicial powers over civic and legal matters concerning the Greek population.

Christians within the Ottoman Empire often were grateful to their Turkish masters and seldom rose up against them. When Macarios, Patriarch of Antioch, went to Moscow on a Church mission in the seventeenth century, he witnessed one of the many massacres that the Roman Catholic Poles had conducted against Eastern Orthodox Russians. "We all wept much," he wrote to his parishioners, "over the thousands of martyrs who were killed by those impious wretches, the enemies of the faith. . . . O you infidels! O you monsters of impurity! O you hearts of stone! . . . [The Poles] have shown themselves more debased and wicked than the corrupt worshipers of idols, by their cruel treatment to Christians, thinking to abolish the very name of Orthodox. *God perpetuate the Empire of the Turks forever and ever!*" The co-operation of the priesthood helped the Turks rule İstanbul and the rest of the former Byzantine Empire with little resistance from within.

Mehmet II was to İstanbul what Constantine I had been to Constantinople. Like his Christian predecessor, the Sultan did not reign during his city's most glorious times, but he established a custodial attitude toward the city's institutions that set a precedent for his successors. Traditionally, Moslem nations, and most particularly the Ottoman, with their nomadic tradition, did not recognize municipal institutions. The city itself was regarded as a necessary commercial and administrative center, but it

A rarity in the Moslem world—a coeducational classroom—is the subject of the Persian manuscript illustration at left. Overseen by a bearded master, some students read, others write, and one boy has his heels beaten with a rod.

never was a corporate entity: in other words, there were no "citizens" of a city, and nothing separated city people from the empire's rural subjects. (The exception was the holy Moslem city of Mecca.)

In this respect Mehmet departed from tradition. Perhaps he was announcing his intention to do so when he undertook to rebuild Hagia Sophia. Although the Sultan added a minaret, which converted the great structure from a church to a mosque, he essentially retained the familiar shape of the edifice. While it was true that Mehmet wanted a new city, he also wanted one that was an enlargement of —not a replacement for—Constantinople.

In 1462 the Sultan restated his intention to make his capital city a cultural center by erecting a fine new mosque —the Mosque of the Fourth Hill. Like many important mosques, Mehmet's was a complex of buildings consisting of a court for worship, several university buildings, and dormitories. *Medreses*—the schools—often were affixed to mosques, but Mehmet determined that the İstanbul *medreses* would become the principal learning center of all Islam. He ordered the best teachers and most talented students in his realm to occupy his Court of Learning at İstanbul.

Finally, Mehmet solidified the power of the Sultan, restricted the power of a potentially competitive aristocracy,

123

and helped to prevent the possibility of a popular uprising against the Sultanate, by strengthening the institution known as the Janissaries.

The Janissaries were a corps that served the Sultanate as a civil service as well as a military guard. Their ranks were filled by children born of Christian parents, especially those living in the Balkans. The child would be removed from his family, converted to Islam, and raised in the *medreses* with special privileges and free education. He was taught the fundamentals of warfare, religion, government; above all else he was taught to honor allegiance to no one but the Sultan. Though not properly an aristocracy, the Janissaries did become a classless arm of the power structure. Moreover, the strict education of the conscripted young boys taught them to take the ethics of the Moslem religion much more seriously than did the general population. The result was a fraternity of extremely polite, self-controlled, thrifty, and courageous youths who did not drink, whose habits of cleanliness were almost excessive, and who were prepared to lay down their lives for their religion or state.

By the early 1500's, the Golden Horn—guarded by the Janissaries—was host to the comings and goings of ships of all nations, and the hills behind it were busy, if not teeming, with commercial and community activities. İstanbul was a prosperous, cosmopolitan city; the orderliness of its government, its traditions, and its beautiful location made an atmosphere conducive to rapid and exciting development. All that was needed was an ambitious and grandiose leader to bring it to life.

He became Sultan in 1520. His name was Suleiman, and he would earn quickly the designation of "the Magnificent." He conquered Rhodes in 1522 and controlled the eastern Mediterranean. He took much of Hungary and threatened all of central Europe by mid-decade. His raids into the West extended across North Africa; he took southern Arabia, and in the 1550's, drove deep into Persia. He unsuccessfully besieged Vienna, attempted to disrupt the Portuguese fleet in the Indian Ocean, and raided Malta. That he did not always seize and occupy his targets did not mean that he was beaten. Seizure and occupation were not always his style. He sometimes preferred simply to keep all his enemies off balance while strengthening his rule in his own territory. He preferred the quick strike to the prolonged siege, and he preferred loot to territory.

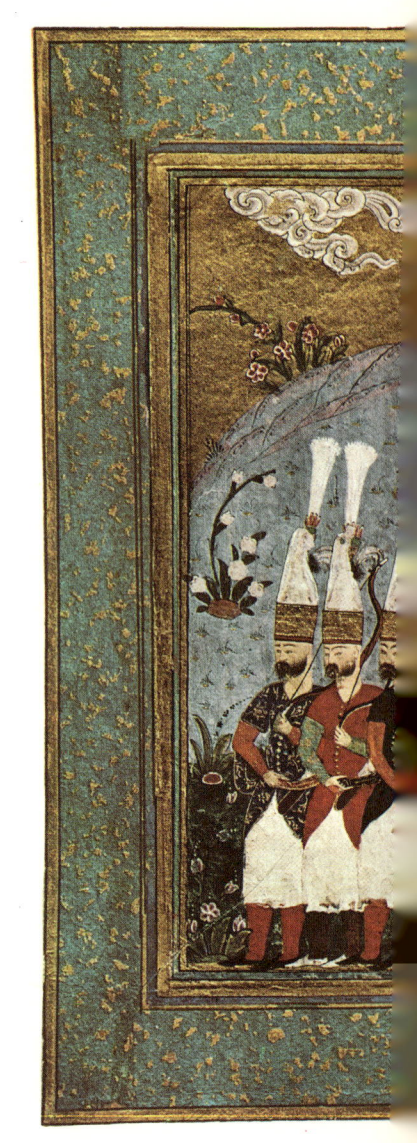

Suleiman continuously entered, departed from, and re-entered İstanbul with great pomp, on his way to or from some monumental battle. It was not unusual for him to bring whole armies home with him for the people of his capital to see. An Englishman, Anthony Jenkinson, once witnessed and recorded one of Suleiman's processions on his way to battle:

There marched before the Grand *Signior*, otherwise called the Great Turke [Suleiman], 6,000 . . . light horsemen, very braue, clothed all in scarlet.

After marched 10,000 men, called *Nortans*, which be tribu-

The Turkish princes depicted in the sixteenth-century miniature above are well protected on their ride by a pair of pages and six Janissary bowmen.

The Venetian drawing above shows Suleiman the Magnificent, one of the most ambitious and successful of the Ottoman sultans, leading a procession of Janissaries. Although Suleiman was known primarily as a warrior, he also was a sophisticated patron of the arts.

taries to ye Great Turke, clothed all in yellow veluet and hats of the same, of the Tartarie fashion, two foote long, with a great robe of the same colour about their foreheads. . . .

After them marched foure Captaines, men of armes, called in Turkish *Saniaques*, clothed all foure in crimson veluet, euerey one hauing vnder his banner twelue thousand men of armes, well armed with their morrions [helmets] vpon their heads, marching in good order, with a short weapon by their sides. . . .

After came sixteen thousand Janizaries, called the slaves of the Grand Signoir, all afoote, . . . in violet silk . . . .

After this there came 1,000 pages of honour, all clothed in cloth of golde, the halfe of them carrying harquebushes, and the other halfe Turkish bowes, with their trusses of arrowes, marching in good order. . . .

After them came seuen pages of honour in cloth of siluer, vpon seuen white horses, which horses were couered with cloth of siluer, all embrodered and garnished with pretious stones, emerauds, diamonds, and rubies most richly.

After them also came six more pages of honour, clothed in cloth of golde, euery one hauing his bowe in his hand, and his fawchine of the Turks fashion by his side.

Immediately after them came the Great Turke himselfe, with great pompe & magnificence, vsing in his countenance and gesture a wonderful maiestie, hauing onely on each side of his person one page clothed with cloth of golde: he himselfe was mounted vpon a goodly white horse, adorned with a robe of cloth of golde, embrodered moste richly with the most pretious stones, and vpon his head a goodly white tuck, containing in length by estimation fifteene yards, which was of silke and linen wouen together . . . and in the toppe of his crowne a little pinnach of white Ostrich feathers, and his horse most richly apparelled in all points correspondent to the same.

After him followed six goodly young Ladies, mounted vpon fine white hackneis, clothed in cloth of siluer, which were of the fashion of mens garments, embrodered very richly with pearle, and pretious stones, and had vpon their heades caps of Goldsmiths worke, hauing great flackets of heare hanging out on each side, died red as blood, and the mailes of their fingers died of the same colour, euery of them hauing two eunuches on each side. . . .

After marched the Great Basha, cheefe conductor of the whole armie, clothed with a robe of Dollymant crimson, and vpon the same another short garment very rich, and about him fiftie Janizaries afoote, of his owne gard, all clothed in crimson velvet. . . .

Then after ensued three other Bashas, with slaues about them, being afoote, to the number of three thousand men. . . .

The camels which carried munition and victuals for the said armie, were in number 200,000.*

*From *Istanbul and the Civilization of the Ottoman Empire*, by Bernard Lewis. Copyright 1963 by the University of Oklahoma Press.

The Sultan was a free-spending patron of the arts, and he attracted men of talent and ambition from everywhere in Islam. Poets, scholars, artists, architects, religious leaders, and merchants converged on the city to take advantage of Suleiman's generosity and to take part in the Moslem cultural boom.

It is revealing that after Suleiman himself, two of the most influential men in İstanbul during his reign were a poet and an architect. The poet, Baki, set the intellectual tone of the city after his friendship with the Sultan began

Designed around a pair of large emeralds and a ruby, the jewel-encrusted ornament at left adorned the turban of Sultan Suleiman.

in 1555: under his influence, it became a romantic place, filled with people who studied poetry and literature as a recreation, with lovers who began writing rhymes to each other as a basic part of courtship. The architect, Sinan, rebuilt almost every important building in the city and added three hundred twelve new structures. One of his masterpieces was the Suleimaniye, a mosque of matchless splendor.

Suleiman died in 1566 while fighting in Hungary. His heart was buried on the battlefield, and his body was taken back to İstanbul for burial in the Suleimaniye. His friend Baki eulogized him:

> The day is born. Will not the lord of the world
>   awake from sleep?
> Does he not show himself from his pavilion,
>   that is like the heavens?
>
> Our eyes are on the roads, no word has come
> From the place where lies the dust beneath the threshold
>   of his majesty.
>
> The colour of his cheek has gone, he lies dry-lipped
> Like a fallen rose apart from the rose water.
>
> Sometimes the Emperor of the skies hides behind the
>   curtain of cloud,
> When he remembers your grace he sweats with shame
>   from the cloud.
>
> This is my prayer: all those who do not weep for you,
>   Young and old, may their tears be buried in the ground.
>
> May the sun burn and blaze with the fire of your parting;
> In grief for you, let him dress in black weeds of cloud.
>
> Weeping tears of blood as it recalls your skill,
> May your sword plunge into the ground from its scabbard.
>
> May the pen tear its collar in grief for you,
> The standard rend its shirt in affliction.*

Under Suleiman and his immediate successors, the educational system in İstanbul was among the soundest in the world. Even the smallest villages in the empire followed the İstanbul example and provided schools in which every young male was given a solid introduction to grammar, syntax, logic, metaphysics, philology, science, rhetoric, geometry, and astronomy. All young people of position and all who aspired to position were expected to be at least

ARMORY, TOPKAPI PALACE, ISTANBUL: PHOTO, ARA GULER

Suleiman's countless conflicts were waged under his golden battle standard, above. More often than not, it led him to victory.

*From *Istanbul and the Civilization of the Ottoman Empire*, by Bernard Lewis. Copyright 1963 by the University of Oklahoma Press.

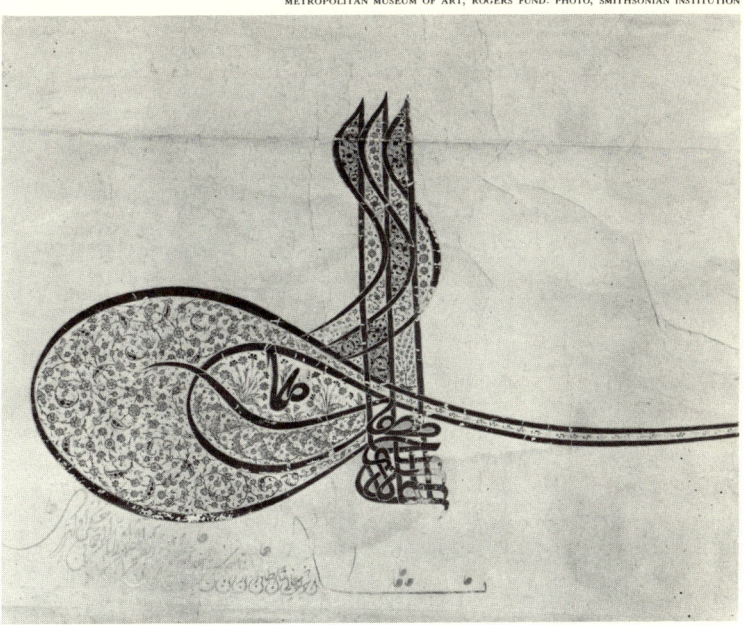

A major art form in Islam, calligraphy had an important governmental function, too. The elaborate design above was Suleiman's official signature and appeared on all state documents. Understandably, a professional calligrapher, not the Sultan himself, executed it.

passable poets, composers of love songs, or discoursers on theology.

Western visitors to Ottoman İstanbul almost invariably were impressed with the good manners and articulateness of the people, especially the young. Many noted that few of the city's residents ever appeared to lose their composure, whatever the circumstances. And a great many observers also commented on the graveness and dignity of the people. Everyone seemed so serious at all times: the children were not even boisterous, the young seldom were rowdy. There was very little crime, and everyone appeared to live with great temperateness. This is a difficult phenomenon to explain: the discipline imposed by the Moslem religion had a great deal to do with it; but the efficiency of the bureaucracy—which created a city in which almost everything operated smoothly and in which, therefore, the unexpected seldom happened—may have been responsible, too. It also is possible, of course, that the Westerners mistook contemplativeness and serenity for somberness.

In some respects, İstanbul under the Ottoman resembled Constantinople. The architecture was rather Oriental in character; Byzantine architecture had grown increasingly Oriental after the time of Justinian. The rich still lived in townhouses high on the hills and in villas along the seashore. The contrast between rich and poor still was striking, as it was in cities all over the world. One Western

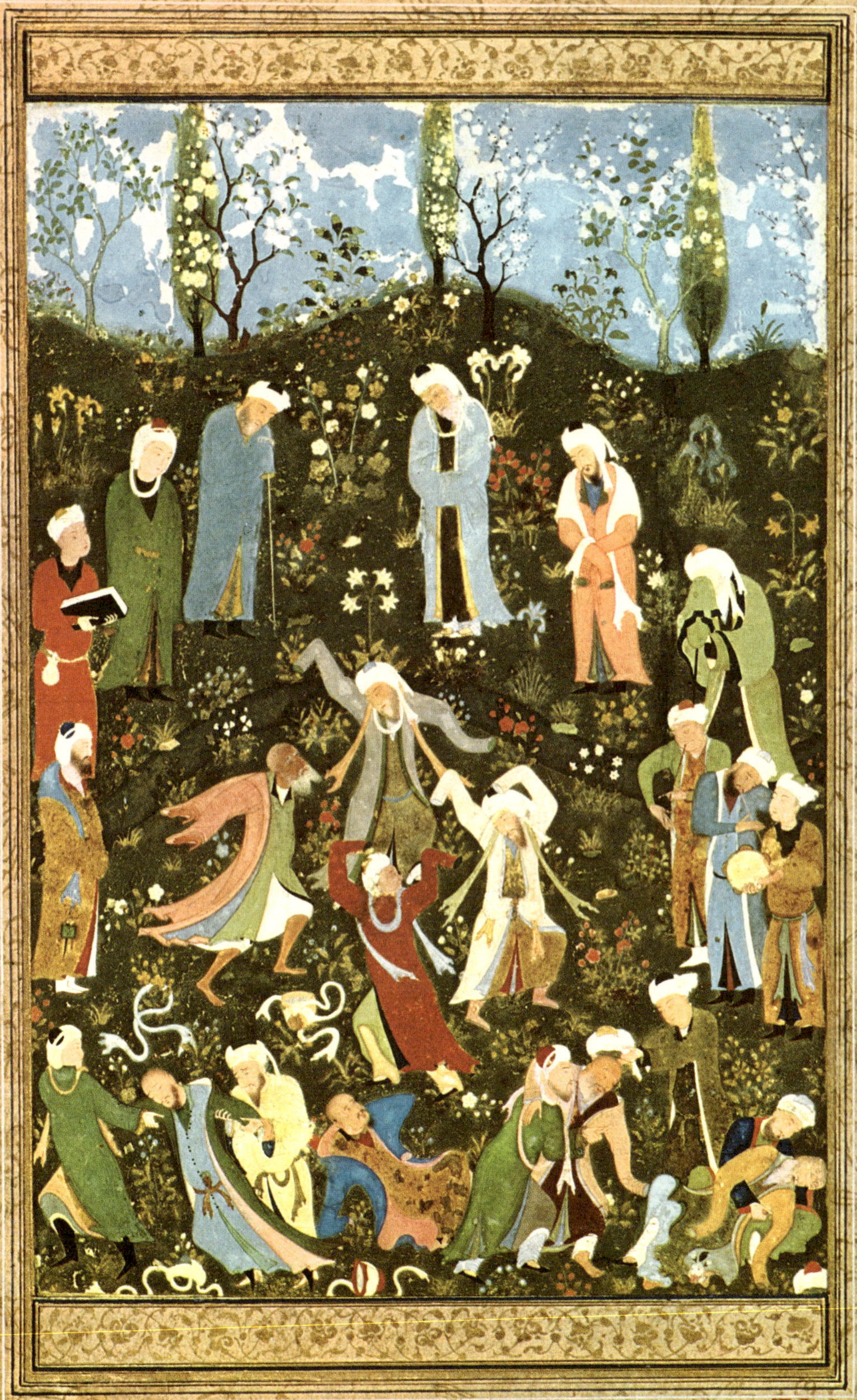

visitor did report, however, that he found the Greek peasantry of the empire to be the best-housed, best-fed, and best-clothed peasants he ever had seen.

Guilds prospered in İstanbul. In the seventeenth century more than seven hundred professional organizations were registered. The guilds were quite competitive—for example, there were separate guilds for carpenters, cabinetmakers, and woodcarvers—and very often they sought the same men for membership. During a procession on a seventeenth-century equivalent of the modern Labor Day, a fight broke out between rival guilds that lasted three full days.

İstanbul consisted of four administrative units: the center of old Constantinople; Galata across the Golden Horn; Eyüp, at the northern end of the Horn beyond the city gates; and Üsküdar, across the Bosporus. İstanbul proper contained the Topkapı Palace, the old Hippodrome Square with Hagia Sophia, Mehmet's palace, and the Suleimaniye, and a great bazaar. Galata, which long had been a favorite stopping place for Genoese merchants and sailors, remained a European-oriented commercial and diplomatic center. The beautiful residences of the European diplomats were situated there, as was an Ottoman school and a convent for dancing dervishes. (The dervishes were a religious order that believed that certain rituals would produce a profound trance through which direct contact with Allah could be achieved.) Üsküdar, which had been a Moslem city before Constantinople fell to the Turks, was a religious center with several mosques and convents—one for howling dervishes.

The defense of İstanbul was maintained by a fleet along the coast and a military patrol on land. Each of the four districts was run by a separate bureaucracy and had separate leadership. One official was charged with the responsibility of maintaining morality and decency in each of the districts; he also was supposed to inspect the quality of goods on sale and to regulate prices.

One of the great controversies of Ottoman İstanbul was whether liquor, tobacco, and coffee were to be permitted. During most reigns the law was against their sale, but the law generally was ignored. In 1633 Sultan Murad IV not only decided to enforce the law, but also had several coffee-drinkers and smokers executed.

OVERLEAF: *This sixteenth-century illustration shows İstanbul (to the right of the Golden Horn) and its suburb Galata during the reign of Suleiman. Although the proportions are distorted, many landmarks—the old Hippodrome at the upper right, Hagia Sophia to the left of the Column of Constantine—are distinguishable. It is not clear, however, whether the ships in the Golden Horn are saluting a homebound or departing fleet or are firing at an enemy.*

UNIVERSITY LIBRARY, ISTANBUL: SKIRA

In the Persian painting opposite, the dancing dervishes—members of a Moslem religious order—whirl to exhaustion in their famous ritual dance.

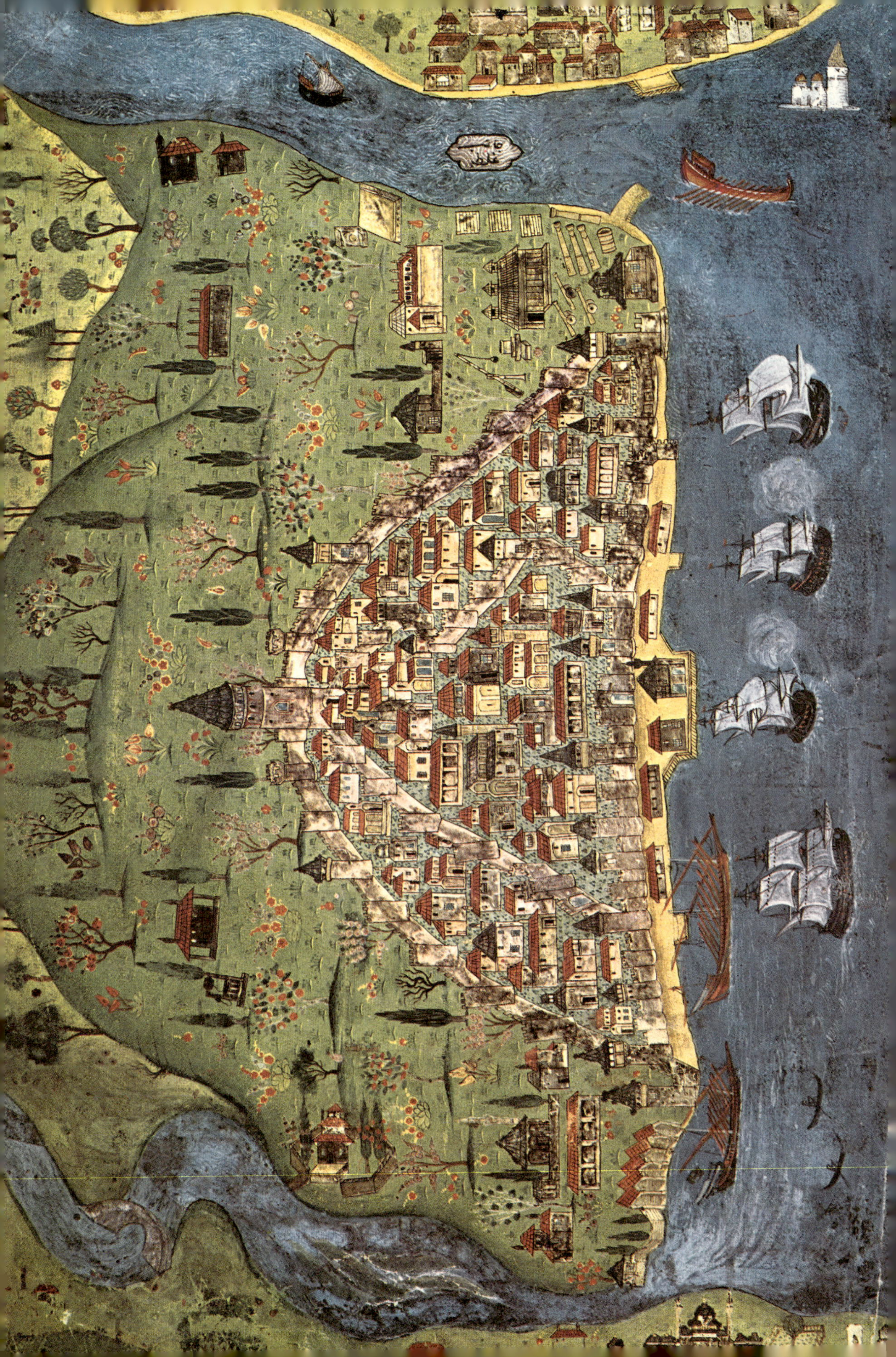

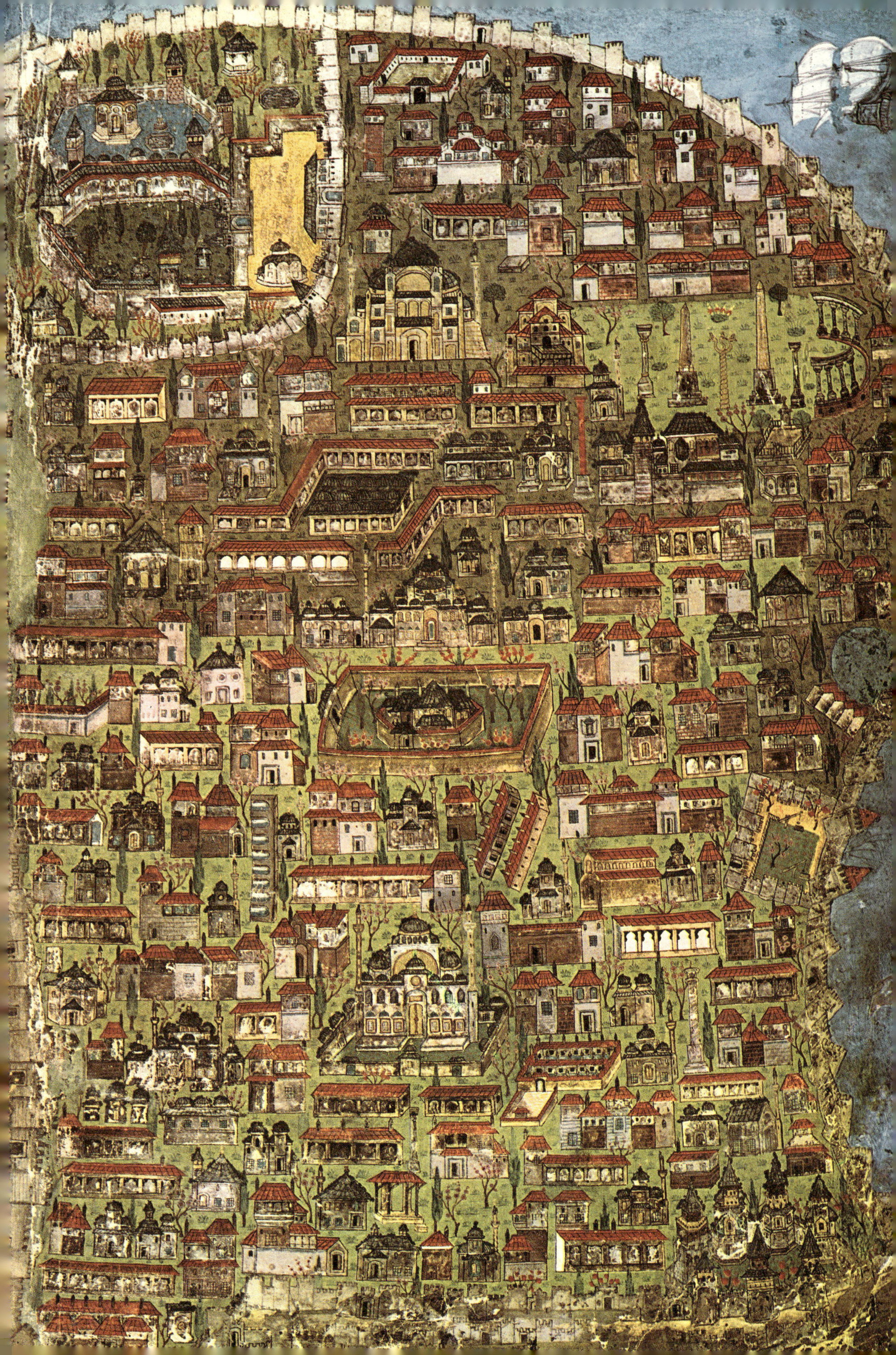

None of Suleiman's successors equaled his strong and grandiose reign. The empire that he had built, however, and its capital, were solid enough to endure and prosper for a century after his death. İstanbul, in all that time, was untouched by war, unruptured by internal uprising.

The trouble was slow in coming. It came in part from Europe and in part from within.

With the Renaissance an extraordinary period of international trade began. It was, of course, the search for new trade routes to the East that had led to the discovery of the New World in 1492. For a while the rich nations of Europe toyed with America—some more earnestly than others—but the importance of the old trade routes never was completely forgotten. Nor was the importance of Istanbul ignored: it still was the city at the center of the world. But no one bothered İstanbul in the sixteenth century because, very simply, the strength of the Ottoman Turks was too great.

In the seventeenth and eighteenth centuries, however, the Ottomans' internal decline allowed the Europeans to begin making slight inroads into the Turkish Empire. Giant Russia, in particular, stared down the Ottoman throat from across the Black Sea. The Sultans were kept busy asserting their strength against European intrusions in the Mediterranean, and against the nationalistic tides in Greece and the Balkans, and had little time for the glorification of İstanbul. Midway through the 1600's the Sultans habitually removed themselves from the conduct of public affairs in order to concentrate on military matters. In their place, appointed viziers took charge of the city and the affairs of the province.

Under the viziers the business of government became a game of intrigue and corruption and self-service. The neglected provinces began to stir with discontent. The taxes in İstanbul began to be spent more for the maintenance of harems and courts than for the public good.

Early in the nineteenth century the weak, corrupt Ottoman Empire began to split at its seams. Even the Janissaries, whose unity and fidelity to the sultan had been a key to the sultans' strength, began to divide—old against young, reformer against antireformer. In 1807, for example, the older Janissaries dealt with the reforming spirit of Sultan Selim III directly: they assassinated him.

Meanwhile, the Greek subjects in the empire, goaded by their Patriarch, planned to regain their freedom and even, eventually, to retake Constantinople. In 1821 the

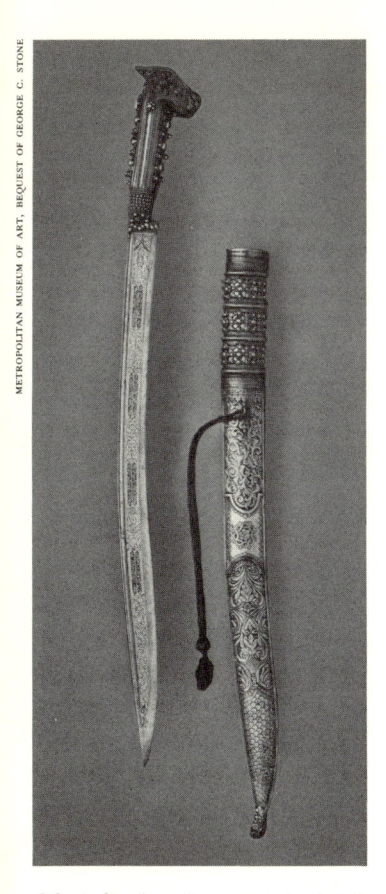

Most Janissaries went to battle armed with a yataghan—a long, slightly curved knife. The yataghan above, about two and a half feet in length, has a handle and sheath made of silver and coral.

Greeks in Rumania, a Turkish tributary, rebelled and began a chain of rebellions by Greeks throughout the western parts of the empire. Although the Sultan promptly crushed the Rumanian rebellion, others sprang up. When some Greeks in Peloponnesus attacked and massacred every Turk they could find, Sultan Mahmud II responded by executing the Orthodox Patriarch in İstanbul. This act caused Russia to sever relations with Turkey, claiming that the execution was an insult to the Orthodox Church. Although the Sultan retook the Greek peninsula, Russia, France, and England—all three interested in securing Mediterranean sailing rights—formed an alliance to help the Greek nationalists. Confronted with this array of power, Sultan Mahmud II agreed to negotiate a settlement with the Greeks. The resulting Treaty of Adrianople in 1829 freed the western Greeks and established a Greek kingdom on the mainland.

Mahmud already had decided to become a reformer. He went about it strangely, to be sure—in 1826 he had executed the majority of the Janissaries in order to demonstrate that he was off to a fresh start. He hired French and Prussian instructors to train his new army. Establishing a land-reform program in the provinces and increasing individual rights, the Sultan curtailed the power of the viziers, discarded the turban as a national headgear and replaced it with the more youthful fez. His son Abdul Medjid, who became Sultan in 1839 and ruled until 1861, continued the reforms, lowering taxes, establishing a council of justice, abolishing trialless capital punishment, and instituting universal laws and penalties.

The reforms worked for a while, and the internal dissension quieted somewhat. Meanwhile, England and France began to regard the Turkish Empire as a European power, since its basic commerce involved importing and exporting goods between East and West. Much interested in maintaining a balance of power in Europe, the French and English even sided with Turkey in its next dispute with Russia. In the Crimean War, which arose from that dispute, Turkey fought alongside its European allies.

The empires commanded from the city behind the Golden Horn never had done well looking to the West. But in the nineteenth century, with the West undergoing an Industrial Revolution, which the Turks did not fully understand—but which they feared—they allowed themselves to be drawn into European political situations. It was to prove a fatal mistake.

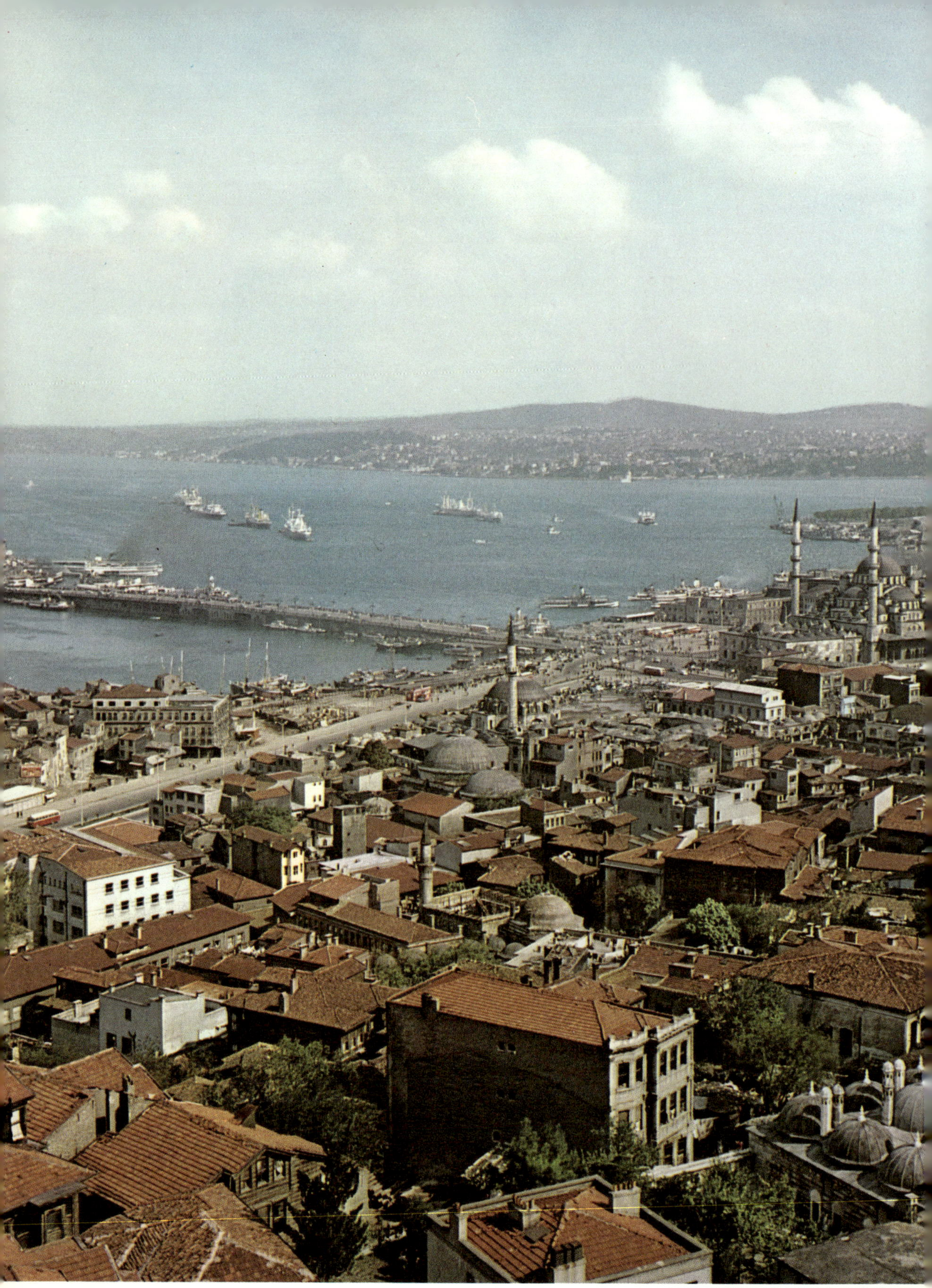
PHOTO RESEARCHERS, INC., NEW YORK: PHOTO, MOTTAR

VIII

İSTANBUL

The fabric of the Ottoman Empire always had been loosely woven. Regionalism, religion, and politics long had divided the various subjects of the realm. Only the strength of the sultan, embodied in his military forces, had held together the warp and woof of the empire.

In the last quarter of the nineteenth century the fabric was wearing thin. The sultan during that period was Abdul Hamid II, who became ruler in 1876. In many ways he was the last sultan sufficiently powerful to effect the radical changes that might have arrested the empire's disintegration. Unfortunately, Abdul Hamid himself personified the contradictions that were destroying the empire. He seemed to acknowledge the need for reform to proceed. For example, in the years of his elevation to the sultanate Abdul Hamid endorsed a new constitution that provided certain democratic guarantees to the individual citizen and called for an elected parliament. But within a year he dissolved the parliament, suspended the constitution, and exiled or jailed the liberals who had pressed the reforms. Shortly thereafter he created a secret police to crush free debate, and he established a despotic one-man rule. He was able to deal so ruthlessly with the opposition because the opposition was divided.

Among the reform elements in the empire were groups that wanted a new government identified with the Moslem religion, other groups that favored a pluralistic state with many religious constituencies, and still others that conceived of a redrawn empire consisting of all peoples who spoke a Turkish dialect. Abdul Hamid employed this division to retain control: by granting special privileges and con-

The harsh misrule of Sultan Abdul Hamid II, pictured above in 1894, stirred the revolutionary activities of the Young Turks.

İstanbul today is both a modern industrial city and a repository of antiquities. Spanned by the Galata Bridge, the Golden Horn now is a harbor only for small boats; larger vessels dock on the shores of the Bosporus.

cessions, he managed to keep the opposition divided. But the fact remained that the sultanate was opposed.

The West took advantage of the internal troubles of the sultanate. Russia, for instance, assumed the role of protector of the Turks' Balkan provinces. When the constitution of 1876 failed to grant these provinces the degree of autonomy that they, with Russian encouragement, demanded, the Russians sent an army through the Balkans and a Black Sea fleet down the Bosporus. The result was the Russo-Turkish War of 1877–78. Despite fierce Turkish resistance, the Russians advanced steadily to the walls of İstanbul. Just as they were about to seize the city, the English—fearful of growing Russian strength in the Near East—sent a fleet through the Dardanelles and commanded the Russians to halt. At the subsequent Berlin Conference the European powers proceeded to carve up the Ottoman Empire. After Russia and Great Britain had claimed a number of Turkish provinces for themselves, they created several new independent states in the Balkans, reducing Ottoman strength in Europe.

It was the Russo-Turkish War that gave Abdul Hamid the excuse to suspend the new constitution, which remained suspended for the rest of the century. The Sultan ruled with an iron fist, sending spies into all places where men congregated, exiling and executing thousands of suspected and actual rebels. The more he repressed them, the faster the secret societies grew, especially in İstanbul. The most effective and best-organized society was the Committee of Union and Progress, known as the Young Turks.

In 1908 the Young Turks staged a rebellion with the help of an army of Turkish subjects from Thessalonica. As the army positioned itself around İstanbul, their spokesmen demanded restoration of the constitution of 1876. Abdul Hamid agreed: elections were held and a constitutional government was established. But when the Thessalonicans went home in 1909, the Sultan attempted a counterrevolution. The army returned quickly to İstanbul, and Abdul Hamid was escorted into exile. His brother Mehmet V was placed on the throne in 1909. He was to be, the Young Turks made it clear, a figurehead: through their National Assembly they themselves were to be in charge.

The Young Turk Revolution essentially ended the reign of the Ottoman sultans. It might have been a good revolution: its leaders were well educated, liberal, and quite anxious to have Turkey join in the progress of the technology-minded West. But it was not to be. Events and several

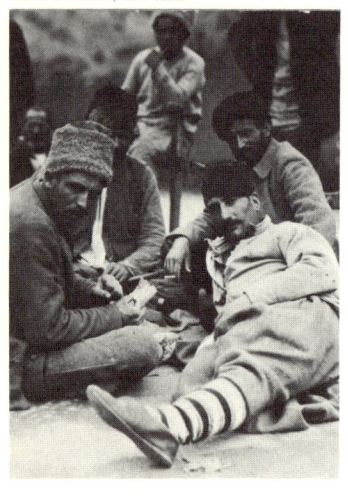

Tough but relaxed, the confident Young Turks above pose in the streets of İstanbul after one of the uprisings that ultimately led to the downfall of the sultanate.

centuries of inept leadership worked against it.

First there were the Balkan wars of 1912–13. During these conflicts the empire's former Greek and Bulgarian subjects seized much of the Ottoman's remaining territory in Europe. Then came World War I itself. Among European nations, Germany had given the most aid to Turkey: it had financed a railroad across Anatolia; it had sent officers to train Turkish soldiers; it had provided loans and advice to the Young Turk leaders. Understandably, the Turks allied themselves with Germany in the war. Although they fought fiercely and well, the ultimate defeat of the Central Powers meant the defeat of the Turks.

After the war İstanbul was occupied by the Allies. The Turks were permitted to retain their Sultan—Mehmet VI, who inherited the throne in 1918—but the Ottoman Empire virtually was dissolved. The Young Turks assembled in Anatolia, which was invaded, with implied Allied approval, by the Greeks in 1920. Mustafa Kemal, one of the most successful Turkish generals during the war (although he had opposed Turkish participation in it), met with a group of friends and former Young Turks in the city of Ankara and formed a National Assembly. Then, under its authority, he rode from village to village stirring up the Turkish population and mobilizing Turkish veterans to resist the Greek assault. It promptly became clear to the Allies that the Sultan's İstanbul government was impotent to deal with the Anatolian Turks. Moreover, when the Turks drove the Greeks from Anatolia in 1922 (and in fact defeated them in a number of engagements in the south and west of Asia Minor), the Allies decided not to stand by their tacit endorsement of the Greek invasion. They decided instead to recognize the independence of the Turkish nation.

When the Allies invited both the Sultan and Kemal to attend the peace conference at Lausanne, they ensured the end of the sultanate. Earlier, not all the Assembly leaders had wanted an end to the monarchy. But the Greek war effectively had demonstrated the impossibility of a coalition: the Sultan in İstanbul and the assembly in Ankara were past and future, irreconcilable.

Actually, no one was absolutely sure when the final schism came. There were men in the Assembly who wanted to found a constitutional monarchy. There were others—Kemal among them—who wanted to do away with the sultanate, replace İstanbul as capital, eliminate everything old, and start anew. But even Kemal hesitated—he did not want to make a martyr of Mehmet VI.

In this World War I cartoon from England, the German Kaiser uses Turkey as ammunition. Although the Turks fought brilliantly and lost few battles, their alliance with Germany proved to be costly.

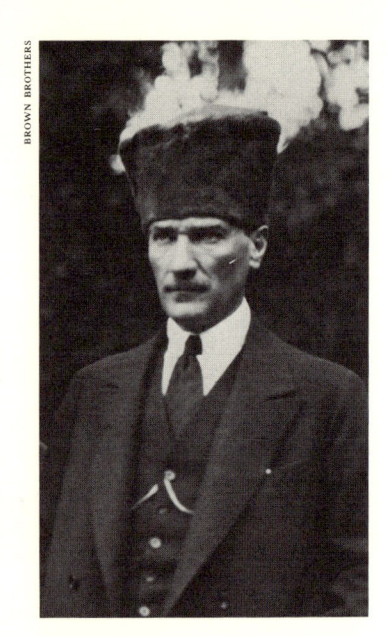

Called Atatürk—"Father of the Turks"—Mustafa Kemal led Turkey from its chaotic birth to stability as a modern republic.

In İstanbul the Sultan did not know what to think. The secret police of the nationalists had a firm grip on the city. There were daily arrests. Some of those arrested were the Sultan's friends. But were they being arrested because they were loyal to the Sultan or because they opposed the Assembly? The Sultan did not even know. All he knew was that his staff was deserting him, that his capital was a terrified city, and that he needed protection.

The British said that it was their policy not to take sides in the internal affairs of Turkey but that they would protect the Sultan's life if it became necessary. Nevertheless, the Allies decided the fate of the sultanate the moment they asked both Mehmet VI and a representative of the National Assembly—Kemal—to attend the peace conference. All but the most devoted monarchists were insulted by that. The Sultan, after all, had been the one to surrender to the Allies although the Turks had lost but few battles in the war. The Sultan had endured quietly the occupation of his capital and had done nothing to defend Anatolia. In contrast, it had been the National Assembly that had formed a new nationalist government. It had been the army of Mustafa Kemal that had driven the Greeks from Turkish soil, won the admiration of the Allies, and earned the coming peace treaty. Public opinion raged against the Sultan—how could he take credit for this? (Whether he did or did not try to is uncertain, but to the people it must have seemed as though he did.)

While in Ankara the National Assembly was officially eliminating the sultanate and establishing the Turkish Republic, the Sultan in İstanbul packed his trunks with jewels, revolvers, and other valuables and departed in a British ambulance. A British naval launch ushered his entourage, which included his son, his First Chamberlain, a bandmaster, his doctor, two secretaries, a valet, a barber, and two eunuchs, to the battleship H.M.S. *Malaya*, which set sail for Malta, then to San Remo, where a villa was waiting for him. A month later, one of eunuchs returned to İstanbul to arrange for the transport of the Sultan's less important baggage: his five wives and numerous children.

When the world learned of the Sultan's escape, the response was immediate. The British Embassy in İstanbul received an urgent telegram from a theatrical agent in the United States:

HIPPODROME NEW YORK COULD USE WIVES OF EX-SULTAN KINDLY PUT ME IN TOUCH WITH PARTY WHO COULD PROCURE THEM.

The Assembly was not disturbed by the Sultan's departure: now it would not have to create any martyrs.

In October, 1923, the allied occupation ended, and the Turkish Republic was born; Kemal was its first president. Later he would be proclaimed "Atatürk" by the Assembly —"Father of Turks." Ankara was his capital.

İstanbul no longer was the capital of anything, but of course, it was affected greatly by the reforms of Atatürk. Profoundly interested in pushing Turkey forward into the twentieth century, Kemal established an electoral dictatorship and ruthlessly pressed for his reforms. It cannot be said that he was a good man—he was vain, immoral, and brutal to his enemies—but it must be said that every official measure he enacted was aimed at the betterment of the Turkish people. Unlike most dictators of his time—and he was contemporary with Mussolini and then Hitler—he had no desire for expansion but concentrated his efforts on solidifying a compact, realistically defined state. He declared all Turks equal, guaranteed freedom of speech, the press, and travel, and separated the activities of church and state.

It probably was this last measure that created the greatest change in Turkey. Atatürk felt that Islam was the influence restraining his people, and he eliminated those religious restraints from government. In 1926 he replaced the Moslem code that had served as law with a new civil code based on Swiss law. Polygamy was outlawed; the Western calendar was adopted; Sunday replaced Friday as the day of rest; religious apparel and the fez were outlawed in favor of Western dress. In 1928 the difficult Arabic script was replaced with the Latin alphabet.

In an effort to eliminate class distinctions among his people, Kemal built thousands upon thousands of secular schools to which all children went. Adult education centers were erected in every town to combat illiteracy; and old

Atatürk's reforms were based on Western models. The postage stamp at left commemorates the conversion from Arabic to a Latin alphabet; Kemal himself demonstrates.

and young alike were taught practices of good nutrition and healthful exercise.

Kemal was wise to remove his capital from İstanbul. The old city on the Golden Horn was filled with symbolic reminders of past glories, past tragedies. He wanted a fresh start—nothing to tempt him or a successor to reseek the glory that was Rome, Byzantium, or the Ottoman Empire.

İstanbul remained an international city, old and new, Eastern and Western, religious and secular. Appropriately, Hagia Sophia is neither church nor mosque: it has been designated a museum, belonging to both faiths and to neither. Many other important old buildings have been similarly designated.

But İstanbul is not itself a museum. It is a vital, vibrant, important city, the nation's financial center and major port, the largest city in Turkey and the most cosmopolitan. Today, as centuries ago, İstanbul University remains a point of assembly for students from throughout the Near East. Open-air restaurants, familiar in the city since before the days of Justinian, still are popular and probably more crowded than ever. Peddlers still sing about their wares in the streets, their commercial songs occasionally contrasting with the chanted prayers of Orthodox Christians and Moslems. Ancient bazaars do a brisk business—thanks to a substantial tourist trade, which centers around the city's splendid international hotels.

Many of the walls encircling the old city have disappeared, and as a result, the distinction between city and suburbs has been somewhat blurred. Galata and the old Asian site of Chalcedon now belong more integrally to Greater İstanbul. The Galata Bridge spanning the Golden Horn is crowded at rush hours with pedestrians in Western-style attire. Beneath the approaches to the bridge are countless shops and the dock for the ferryboats that cross the Bosporus and unite the Asian and European sections of the city. Commuters—who are as accustomed to water-travel as many Westerners are to bus, subway, and automobile travel—have ample opportunity to purchase fresh fish for dinner on their way home: Bosporus fishermen bring their boats right up onto the shore of the Golden Horn and peddle their day's catch.

The hills of İstanbul afford splendid views of the intertwining waterways below. Narrow, rectangular, earthen-colored houses of three and four stories are clustered along narrow streets on the hillsides, their squareness contrasting with the gentle curves of the city's hundreds of domed edi-

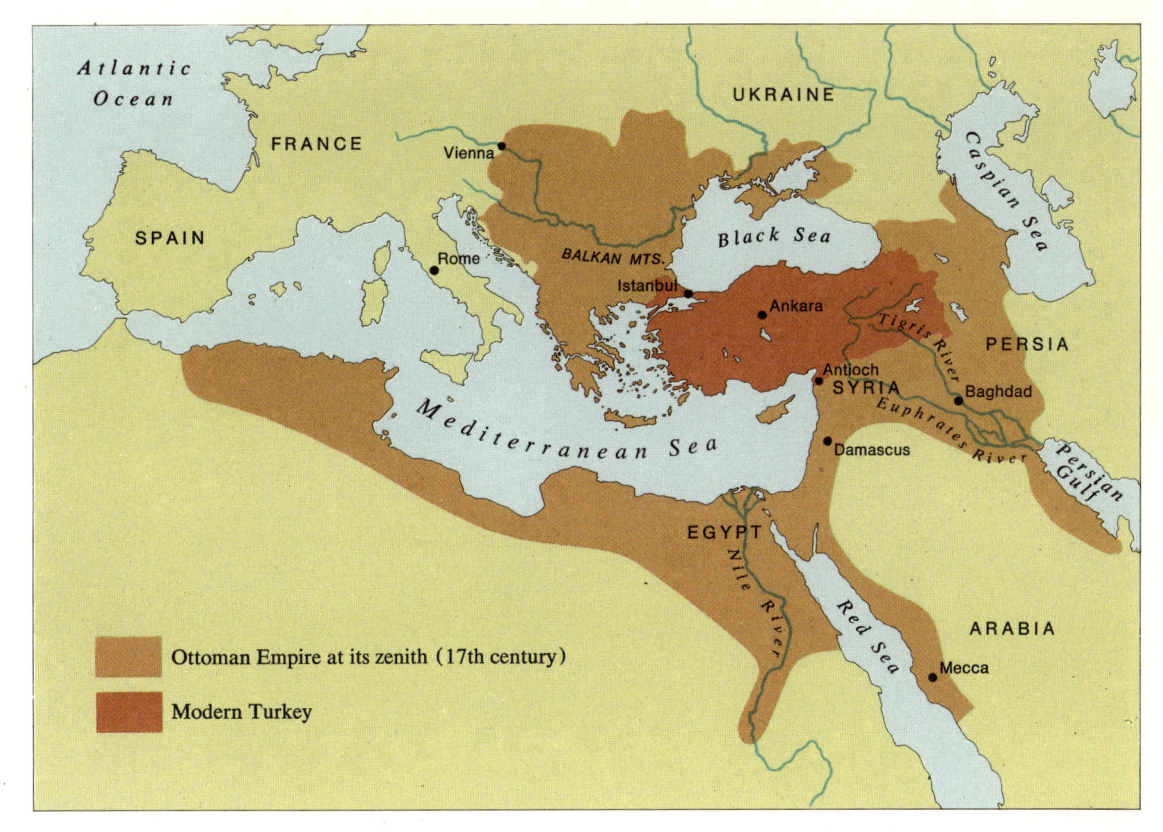

As the map above reveals, modern Turkey is considerably smaller than was the Ottoman Empire at its height. Ankara has replaced İstanbul as capital of the country, which has become a republic.

fices. From almost any point in İstanbul one sees a church or a mosque or two, and rising impressively above the skyline are minarets and crosses.

The Bosporus is lined with suburban homes, parks, and inns. In the Thracian outskirts several age-old cemeteries remain. There the dead of thousands of years of history are interred. History, indeed, is all around. Sections of walls survive, and ancient gates remind residents and tourists of scores of armies from many epochs, marching behind the standards of Caesar, Christ, and Mohammed, singing and chanting in Greek, Latin, or Turkish.

For here in these hills—possibly more often than in any other place on earth—worlds met to either blend or clash. Through these hills West reached East and East headed West. From these hills civilizations radiated. And in a symbolic way İstanbul remains, like Constantinople and Byzantium before it, the city at the center of the world. Below these hills, within sight of them, ships from everywhere still come and go, their many flags rippling in the breath of Boreas as he prances in the Bosporus and the Golden Horn.

143

Ancient-style commerce wakes a street at dawn in modern İstanbul.

The Dolmabahche Palace

144

CITY ON THE GOLDEN HORN

As the sun rises from the Orient, İstanbul fills with the sights and sounds of a past and present rooted in East and West. Modern power plants cough and groan awake. Quick, whistling ferryboats dart from one Bosporus shore to the other. Great freighters, blasting throaty horns and belching black smoke, arrive from all over the world with cargo that capped longshoremen unload and replace with such products as Turkish cigarettes brought right to the docks by long freight trains. Fish from the Black Sea and produce from Mediterranean shores are transported over cobbled streets on clacking, horse-drawn wagons to roadside markets and to the great bazaar, where merchants chant as their ancestors chanted in the Mideastern singsong that strikes both Western European and East Asian visitors as exotic. On one building wall is an old inlay of Arabic script; in a nearby window, a machine giving stock exchange quotations may be seen. Along the waterways are Western-style buildings that once housed Turkish sultans. Scribes, who in another day might have worked for the sultans, now use typewriters and sell their services to illiterate laborers who want to write home. Late in the day breezes mix sea smells with the scents of roasting lamb, Turkish coffee, baklava, and eggplant. Across the water Asia darkens first; then the ancient hills, the domes and minarets that are centuries old, and the modern hotels glow pink as the last light of the Occidental sun filters through the smoky air.

A scribe and his client

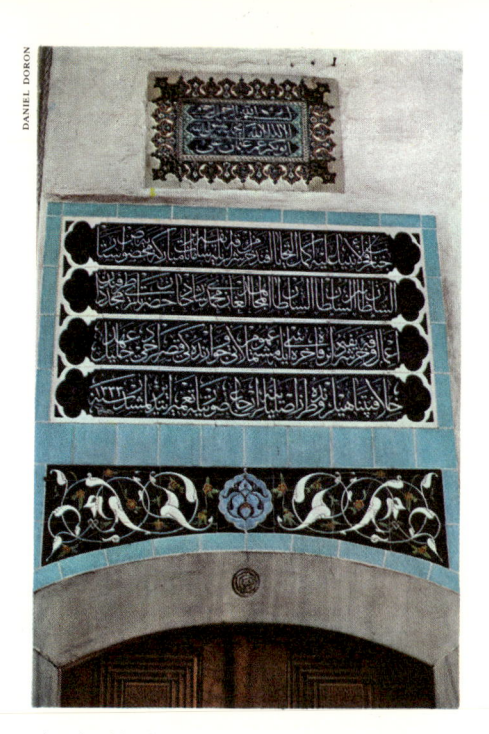

An Arabic inscription on Τοπκαπι Palace

The Bazaar, market place for everything

İstanbul, old and new, silhouetted against the sunset

Made in Constantinople toward the end of the tenth century, the silk cloth at left was sent to France to serve as a shroud for a famed cleric. The eagles—a favorite motif in Byzantine art—are each more than a foot and a half long.

HORIZON CARAVEL BOOKS

KENNETH W. LEISH, *Editor*

Janet Czarnetzki, *Art Director*

Sandra L. Russell, *Copy Editor*

Jessica Bourgeois, *Picture Editor*

Kathleen Fitzpatrick, *Text Researcher*

Gay Sherry, *Text Researcher*

Annette Jarman, *Editorial Assistant*

Gertrudis Feliu, *Chief, European Bureau*

ACKNOWLEDGMENTS

The Editors would like to thank the following individuals and organizations for their valuable assistance:

Dumbarton Oaks Collection, Washington, D.C.—
    Susan Boyd
Ara Guler, İstanbul
Metropolitan Museum of Art, New York

Maps by Francis & Shaw, Inc.

The quotations on pages 112 and 116 are from *Memoirs of the Crusades*, by Geoffrey Villehardouin and Jean, Sire de Joinville (translated by Sir Frank T. Marzials). Dutton Paperback Edition, 1958.

FURTHER READING

Burckhardt, Jacob, *The Age of Constantine the Great*. Doubleday, 1949 (paperback).

Diehl, Charles, *Byzantium: Greatness and Decline*, translated by Naomi Walford. Rutgers University Press, 1957.*

Downey, Glanville, *Constantinople in the Age of Justinian*. University of Oklahoma Press, 1960.

Hürlimann, Martin, *Istanbul*. Thames & Hudson, 1958.

Kinross, Lord, *Ataturk*. Morrow, 1965.

Merriman, Roger B., *Suleiman the Magnificent, 1520–1566*. Cooper Square, 1966.

Ostrogorsky, George, *History of the Byzantine State*. Rutgers University Press, 1957.

Price, M. Philips, *A History of Turkey*. Macmillan, 1956.

Rice, David T., *The Byzantines*. Praeger, 1962.

———, *Constantinople*. Stein and Day, 1965.

Runciman, Steven, *The Fall of Constantinople, 1453*. Cambridge University Press, 1965.

Sherrard, Philip, and the Editors of Time-Life Books, *Byzantium*. Time Inc., 1966.

Stewart, Desmond, and the Editors of Time-Life Books, *Early Islam*. Time Inc., 1967.

Vryonis, Speros, Jr., *Byzantium and Europe*. Harcourt, 1967.*

*Also available in paperback.

INDEX

Boldface indicates pages on which maps or illustrations appear

A

Abdul Hamid II, Sultan, 137–138, **137**
Abdul Medjid, Sultan, 135
Adrianople, 16, 46, 97, 116
Adrianople, Treaty of (*1829*), 135
Adriatic Sea, 111
Aegean Sea, 6
Aeneas, 49
Africa, 31, 60
Ahmed III, Sultan, **6–7**, 7
Alcibiades, 37–38
Alexander (uncle of Constantine VII), 101
Alexandria, 60, 67, **67**, 80
Alexius I, Emperor, 105, 107
Alexius III, Emperor, 111, 114, 115
Alexius IV, Emperor, 114
Allah, 131
Allies (World War I), 139–140
Amastrianum, on map, **72–73**
Anatolia, 18, 29, 42, 105, 107, 139, 140
Anatolian Turks, 22
Anaxibius, Admiral, 38–39
Ankara, 139, 143
   on map, **143**
   National Assembly in, 139–140
Antioch, 102, 107
Aqueduct of Valens, on map, **72–73**
Arabia, 124
Arabic alphabet and script, 141, **141**
Arabs, 6, 88, 93, 98, 102, 104, 105
   army of, 90, **90–91**
   and siege of Constantinople (*717–718*), 89–90
Arcadianae, 71
Arcadius, Forum of, on map, **72–73**
Architecture, Byzantine, 129
   Roman church, 74
   Moslem, 127, 128, 129
   see also specific examples of
Argonauts, voyages of, 28
Argos, 28
Arians, 94, **94**
Armenia, 38, 68, 99

Art, Byzantine, 67, 100
   Moslem, 127
   motifs in, 120, **120**, 121, **121**
Asia Minor, 6, 85, 98, 99, 107, 116
Atatürk, *see* Kemal, Mustafa
Athene Chalcioecus, Temple of, 35–36
Athenian Confederacy, 36
Athenian League, 36
Athens, 6, 32, 33
   rise to power, 36
   wars of, 36–37
   relations with Byzantium, 36–39
Augusta Antonia, 40
Augustaeum, 70
Augustus, defined, 41–42
Avars, 83, 85–86

B

Babylonians, 92
Baghdad, 95
Baki (poet), 127–128
   quoted, 128
Baldwin, Count of Flanders, 113, 116
Balkan Peninsula, 27
Balkan Wars (*1912–1913*), 139
Balkans, 23, 85, 97, 107, 116, 124, 134, 138
Barbarians, 65, **65**, 83, **83**
Bardas, *caesar*, 98, **98–99**, 99
Basil I, Emperor, 97–100
Basil II, Emperor, **96**, 97, **98–99**, 104
Bayazid II, Sultan, 119
Berlin Conference, 138
Bithynia, 39, 40
Black Sea, 6, 19, 28–29, 32, 38, 117, 134, 138, 145
Blue Party, 55–56, 62, 63, 65
Boeotia, 33
Boniface, Marquis of Montferrat, 111
Boreas (north wind), 27, 119, 143
Bosphoria, 32
Bosporus, 6, 18, 19, 29, 30, 32, 36–37, 38, 39, 51, 86, 107, 131, 138, 142, 143, 145
   on map, **20–21**, **108–109**

shores of, **136**, 137
Bulgaria, 97, 102, 104, 117, 139
   army of, 89
Bulgars, 97, 102
Byzantine Empire, 6, 51, **64**, 68, 81, 83, 84, 86, 88, 89, 92, 95, 102, 104, 105, 107, 111, 122, 142
   religious division in, 86
   iconoclasts in, 91
   establishment of Macedonian dynasty in, 100–101, 102
   methods of warfare, 103, **103**, 104, **104**
   decline of, 110, 117
Byzantine style, 67, 83
Byzantium, 6, 27–45 *passim*, 47, 49, 67, 72, 85, 143
   founding and building of, 30–31; government of, 31–32; culture of, 32; Persian capture of, 32–33; Spartan occupation of, 33, 34, 35, 38; as independent city-state, 36; wars of pro-Athens and pro-Sparta forces in, 36–38; repulsion of Macedonian siege, 39; Celtic invasion of, 39–40; Romanization of, 40–41; renamed, 46
Byzas, 30

C

Caesar, defined, 41–42
Cappadocians, 68
Carthage, 85
Celts, 39–40, 68
Central Powers, 139
Chalcedon, 30, 32, 85, 115, 142
   Persian destruction of, 33
   Spartan fortress at, 38
   Fourth General Council at, 77
Charlemagne, Emperor, 95
Christ, 88
   divinity of, 77, 80
Christianity, 51, 68, 86, 92
   evolution and spread of, 43, **44**, 45
   Eastern and Western division in, 12, 43, 45–46, 49–51, 67–68, 77, 93, 102, 111–112, 122
   and Monophysitism, 77, 80–81
   Crusades, 107
   in Moslem İstanbul, 119–120, 122, 124
Chrysopolis, 46
Committee of Union and Progress (Young Turks), National Assembly of, 138–141
Comneni family, 116
Comnenos, Constantine, 116, **116**
Constantia, 43, 46
Constantine I, Emperor, **cover**, 6, 8, 24, 42, 43, **43**, **44**, 45, 47, 50, **50**, 51
   quoted, 49
   conversion to Christianity, 45–46
   and founding of Constantinople, 46, 49, 67, 122
Constantine IV, Emperor, 88
Constantine V, Emperor, 93, **93**
Constantine VI, Emperor, 92, **92–93**, 95
Constantine VII, Emperor, 100–101, **100**
Constantine XI, Emperor, 12–13, 18, 19, 116, 117
Constantine, Forum of, 63, 131, **132–133**
   on map, **72–73**
Constantine, Wall of, on map, **72–73**
Constantinople, 6, 12, 13, 25, 42, 46, 54, 57, 63, 69, 80, 107, 116, 143
   map of, **72–73**
   personification of, 8, **8**, 67, **67**
   ruins of walls of, 25, **25**

150

mosaic model of, 77, **78–79**
founding of, 46, 49, **49**, 51; development of government and economy of, 51–52, 54–56; growth of culture in, 51–52; East and West influences in, 52–53; slavery in, 54; treatment of poor in, 54–55; demes in, 55–56, 59, 62
rule of Justinian and Theodora in, 57, 60–65, 67–81 *passim*; Nika Rebellion in, 61–65, 70; cultural role of, 67, 68; population of, characterized, 68–69; life in, 69–70; rebuilding of, 70–71, 74; laws of, 74, 76–77; effect of split in Christianity on, 81
as Christian capital (*565–843*), 83–95; under Justin II, 83–84; revolt of demes in, 84–85; invasion by Avars, 85–86; under Heraclius, 85–86, 88; Arab siege of (*678*), 88–90; under Leo III and iconoclast emperors, 89–93, 95; army of, 90, **90–91**
under Michael III and Macedonian emperors, 97–102; Bulgar assault on, 97; Russian attacks on, 102, 104; disorders in, 104–105; threatened by Seljuk Turks, 105, 107; Crusade assaults on, 107, **108–109**, 110–112, **112–113**, 113, 114–117
Moslem threat to, 14, 18; Turkish siege of (*1453*), **10**, 11–25 *passim*, 119; Turkish capture of, 22, 23, 24–25, 74, 131; Moslem control of, 119–124 *passim* compared to İstanbul, 129, 131
Constantinople, University of, 100
Constantius, *caesar*, 42, 43
Copts, 68
Court of Learning, 123
Crete, 98, 104
Crimean War, 135
Crusades, map of, 107, **108–109**
First, 106, **106**, 107
Fourth, 6, 110–112, **112–113**, 113–116
currency of, 111, **111**
Cyprus, 67, **67**, 102
Cyrene, King of, 31, **31**

D
Dandolo, Enrico, 110
Danube River, 97, 104
Dardanelles, 6, 19, 39–40, 138
Darius I, King of Persia, 32–33
Dark Ages, 51
Delacroix, Eugène, painting by, **112–113**
Demes, 55–56, 62–63, 65
Dervishes, **130**, 131
Diocletian, Emperor, 40, **40**, 41–43, 45
Dolmabahçe Palace, İstanbul, **144**
Dorian Greeks, 28, **28–29**, 29

E
Easter, celebration of, 53
Eastern Empire, *see* Byzantine Empire
Eastern Orthodox Church, 6, 12–13, 122
see also Christianity
Egypt, 56, 65, 77, 86, 92
England, *see* Great Britain
Europe, 19, 134, 135
Euxine Sea, *see* Black Sea
Exokionion, 51
Eyüp, 131

F
Forum of the Ox, on map, **72–73**
Fourth General Council of the Church (*451*), 77
France, 135
Franks, 111

G
Galata, 20, 112, 115, 131, **132–133**, 142
on map, **72–73**
Galata Bridge, **136**, 137, 142
Galerius, *caesar*, 42
Gaul, 43
Genoa, Italy, 19–20, 21, 117, 131
Germany, 68, 139
cartoon of Kaiser of, 139, **139**

Gibbon, Edward, quoted, 101
God, images of, 92
Godfrey of Bouillon, 107
Golden Gate, 86
on map, **72–73**
Golden Horn, 6, 19, 20, 21, 25, 30, 31, 33, 40, 52, 57, 67, 85, 99, 112, 119, 124, 131, **132–133**, 135, 142
maps of, **20–21**, **72–73**
harbor of, **136**, 137
Goths, 46, 68
Goths, Column of the, on map, **72–73**
Great Britain, 135, 138, 140
Greece, 6, 28, 32, 33, 35, 36, 39, 40, 43, 68, 91–92, 134, 135, 139
explorations and colonies of, 27–31
warriors of, **26**, 27
dominance of, 33
classical tradition of, 51
education of, 52
war with Turkey, 139–140
"Greek fire," 102, 104, **104**
Greek language, 68–69, 77
Greek Orthodox Church, 122, 135
Greek Peninsula, 135
Greeks, nationalism of in Ottoman Empire, 110–120, 122, 131, 134–135
Green Party, 55–56, 62, 63
Gregory II, Pope, 93
Guilds, 52, 131

H
Hagia Sophia, 12, 22, 24, **24**, 70, 71, 74, 77, 83, 85, 131, **132–133**, 142
details of decorations of, 70, **70**, 71
mosaics from, **cover**, 8, 74, **75**, 77, **78–79**
roundels from, 74, **75**
Crusaders' destruction of, 116
becomes a mosque, 25, 123
Hebdomon, 70–71
Hebrews, 92
Helena, mother of Maxentius, **44**, 45
Heraclius, Emperor, 85–86, 88, **88**

The enamel plaques at left and on the next page decorated the crown of Constantine Monomachus, Byzantine Emperor from 1042 to 1055.

BUDAPEST NATIONAL MUSEUM: GIRAUDON

151

Hero, illustrations from *Book of Machines of War* by, 103, **103**
Hippodrome, 55, 57, 63, 83, 84, 85, 89, 131, **132–133**
    on map, **72–73**
    chariot races held at, 59
    and Nika Rebellion, 64–65
Hippodrome Square, 131
Hitler, 141
Holy Apostles, on map, **72–73**
Holy Land, 107, 110, 111
    on map, **108–109**
Holy Roman Empire, 110
Hungary, 97, 124, 128
    cavalry of, **22–23**, 23
Hungary, King of, 111
Huns, 68
Hypatius, 63

I

Iconoclasts, 90–93, 94, 95, 100
Igor, Prince of Kiev, 102
Iliad, 28
Illyrians, 27, 68
Illyricum, 43, 69
Imperial Basilica, 70
    on map, **72–73**
Indian Ocean, 124
Industrial Revolution, 135
Ingerina, Eudocia, 98
Innocent III, Pope, 110
Ionian Greeks, 29
Irene, Empress, 93, **93**, 95
Isaac, Brother of Alexius III, 114–115
Islam, 11, 15, 18, 67, 86, 93, 105, 120, 122, 127, 129, 137, 141
    İstanbul as center of, 123
    conversion of Christians to, 124
    legal code of, 141
İstanbul, 7, 25, 124, 131, **132–133**, 137–145 *passim*
    under Ottoman Turks, 119–124; Christians in, 119–120, 122; growth of, 124; under Suleiman, 124–128, 134; society and culture of, 127–129, 131; dignity of people of, 129; education in, 123, **123**, 128–129; compared to Constantinople, 129, 131; administrative units of, 131; guilds of, 131; government of, 134; decline of, 134–135; secret societies in, 138; Russian advance on, 138; end of sultanate in, 139–141; Allied occupation of, 139; under Kemal, 114–142
    characterized and described, 6, **136**, 137, 142–143, 144, **144–145**, 145, **146–147**, 147
İstanbul University, 142
Italian Peninsula, 43
Italy, 65, 67, 104

J

Janissaries, 22, 124, **124–125**, 125, 126, **126**, 134, 135
    yataghan of, 135, **135**
Jenkinson, Anthony, quoted, 125–127
Jerusalem, 85, 107, 110
Jews, in Moslem İstanbul, 120
John I, Emperor, 102, 104
John the Cappadocian, 63
Justin I, Emperor, 56, 60
Justin II, Emperor, 83–84
Justinian, Emperor, **front endsheet**, 8, 56–57, **57**, **66**, 67, 69, 77, **78–79**, 85, 129, 142
    quoted, 56
    palace of, 62, **62**, **72–73**
    map of conquests of, 64, **64**
    characterized, 56–57; and Theodora, 57, 60–61; government of, 60–65; and Nika Rebellion, 61–65, 70; and rebuilding of Constantinople, 67, 68, 70–71; decree of *528*, 74, 76; and Monophysites, 77, 80–81; death of, 83
Justinian II, Emperor, 88–89
Justinian's Code, 74, 76–77, **76–77**, 100

K

Kemal, Mustafa, 139–142, **140**, **141**
Koran, 119, **119**
    stand for, 122, **122**
Krum, King of the Bulgars, 97

L

Latin alphabet, 141
Lazarus, icon-painter, 95
Leo III, Emperor, 89–93, **93**
    iconoclasm of, 90–91, 93
Leo IV, Emperor, 93
Leo V, Emperor, 94, **94**
Leo VI, Emperor, 101
Leo, son of Basil, imprisonment of, 101, **101**
Leontius, 89
Licinius, 43, **43**, 46
Literature, Moslem, 127–128
Longo, Giovanni Giustiniani, General, 19, 22, 24

M

Macarios, Patriarch of Antioch, quoted, 122
Macedonia, 97
    coins of, 39, **39**
Macedonians, 39, 97
    characterized, 100–101
    in Byzantine Empire, 100–101
Mahmud II, Sultan, 135
Malta, 124, 140
Maps
    siege of Constantinople, **20–21**
    Byzantine Empire, **36–37**
    conquests of Justinian, **64**
    Constantinople, **72–73**
    Crusades, **108–109**
Marathon, Battle of, 32
Marcian, Column of, on map, **72–73**
Marmara, Sea of, 7, 19, 29–30, 70, 71, 88, 107
    on map, **72–73**
Maurice, Emperor, 84–85
Maxentius, 43, **44**, 45
Maximian, *augustus*, 40, **40**, 42, 43
Mecca, 123
Mediterranean Sea, 6, 32, 33, 67, 111, 124, 134, 135, 145
Medreses, 123
Megara, 29, 30, 31, 32
Mehmet II, Sultan, 14, **14**, 74, 117, **118**, 119, 131
    court of, 16, **17**
    caftan of, 120, **120**
    youth and education of, 15–16, 18
    and siege of Constantinople, 18–25 *passim*
    and government of İstanbul, 119–124
Mehmet V, Sultan, 138
Mehmet VI, Sultan, 139–141
Mesembria, 32, 36
Mesopotamia, 38
Michael III, Emperor, 97–99, **98–99**, 101
Michael VIII, Emperor, 117
Middle East, 52, 77, 81, 100, 120
Middle Street, on map, **72–73**
Milan, 43
Milan, Archbishop of, 81
Miletus, 29, 30, 31
Milion Arch, on map, **72–73**
Milvian bridge, 43, 45
Mohacs, Battle of, **22–23**, 24
Mohammed, 67, 86, **87**, 105
    banner of, 11, **11**
Mongolians, 105, 117
Monophysite theology, 77, 80–81, 86, 93
Monotheism, 92
Moscow, 122
Moslems, 11, 14, 21–22, 95, 107, 110
    law of, 86
Mosque of the Fourth Hill, 123
Mourtzuphlos, 115
Murad II, Sultan, 15–16, 18
Murad IV, Sultan, 131
Mussolini, 141
Mycenaean Greeks, 28

N

National Assembly, Turkey, 138–141
Nea Roma, 46
Near East, 138, 142
New Rome, *see* Constantinople
New World, discovery of, 134
Nicaea, Council of, 92, **92–93**
Nicephorus II, 95, 101–102
    assassination of, 89, **89**
Nicholas V, Pope, 12
Nicomedia, 42, 46
Niger, Pescennius, 40
Nika Rebellion, 61–65, 70
Normans, 107
North Africa, 65, 124